SCOTTISH CROSSWORDS BOOK

by BILL RODGER

INTRODUCTION

This book features 60 crosswords with a Scottish theme. Answers to all of the clues are in the form of Scottish place names, personalities, quotations, and words from the Scots language.

They are compiled by Bill Rodger — an Ayr businessman who has been a crossword complier all his adult life.

Besides being a sound test of wits and knowledge of Scotland the crosswords keep alive many marvellous old Scots words which all too sadly are passing from regular daily use in the modern world. A few topical clues relate to conditions at the time of compilation.

"Scottish Crosswords" was published by Lang Syne Publishers Ltd, Old School, Blanefield, Glasgow G63 9HX in 1985 and printed by Waterside Printers.

ISBN: 0 946264 38 2
REPRINTED: 1987, 1987, 1988, 1988, and 1990.

1

ACROSS

1. Carry Tom over the Firth? (8)
5. In a way, surface with a Scots invention? (6)
9. Pull on the oars Mr. Wells! Sprint towards castle near Kilmarnock? (8)
10. Aberdeenshire girl – one of the five that is! (6)
12. A stool up for the wise birds? (6)
13. Lying between Dumbarton and Helensburgh could be an ace for former Scots Secretary? (8)
15. The most westerly part of the Scottish mainland (12)
18. Spean Br? i.e. by the Church of Scotland! (12)
23. Are kilts required to be dressed at Skye's only whisky distillery? (8)
24. See 28.
26. A guy? An upset man in motion? (6)
27. Inclined to be raised (8)
28, 24. "Go, fetch to me a pint o' wine and fill it in a —— ——," (Burns) (6,6)
29. An alias used by Mrs. Agnes Maclehose – an acquaintance of Robert Burns (8)

DOWN

1. Auto off-spring? Royal rider from Stirling! (6)
2. 1984 author standing stones in Fifeshire? (6)
3. Mr. McLeod's mountain? — just a child's favourite marble! (4-3)
4. Scots' busybody of late? (4)
6. . . . and rune can be beneath! (7)
7. Only chum seen in picturesque village on the north coast of the Moray Firth! (8)
8. Cringes round point — it's caused by folding! (8)
11. Earldom of Brechin whose seat is a house of the same name and whose doors were closed permanently in 1715 by the 4th Earl (7)
14. Rent? — 'Tis often coming as a biting blast! (7)
16. Famous Stirling house used for medical purposes, mostly! (8)
17. Faithful fellow getting under tongue! (3,5)
19. Luce Bay's stormy, losing year and becoming common type of Scottish drawbridge! (7)
20. In Scottish football he'll have to step up to become a Junior! (7)
21. Is a son upset at the legendary Gaelic poet? (6)
22. European city to which many early Scots reformationists went to study calvanism (6)
25. Chicken wishbone from a Colibri lighter? (4)

2

ACROSS

1. Reach log floating on west coast inlet? (8)
5. Crazy sprite who is a scorner of the Scots! (6)
9. I remove a sporting centre in Inverness-shire? (8)
10. Surname of the founder of the printing and publishing firm which is responsible for the 'Glasgow Herald' amongst others (6)
11. Future Glasgow hotel perhaps? The council have set their hearts on! (8)
12. Maid gets upset in a little accounts matter — she was designed by Scots architect! (6)
14. Silly circle? Feel about part of the Shetlands for it! (4,2,4)
18. Arm of the North Sea, officially described as 'lying between Tarbat Ness and Lossiemouth!' (5,5)
22. Hoy village upset at being less than New York? (6)
23. The steps rising to the entrance of a kiln — a good place to commit a murder? (4–4)
24. Is the Dunkeld Rink always old? (6)
25. Senior football side who are everyone's 'buddies'? (2,6)
26. Perthshire loch takes a drop, we hear! (6)
27. Send Rona round to fetch first professor of oriental languages at Glasgow University! (8)

DOWN

1. Piece of burnt coal, still in its original shape – what a sight! (6)
2. A liver, otherwise used for spreading yarn? (6)
3. Mad fly seen around the galley? (6)
4. Score a unit on a famous Scottsh golf course? (10)
6. Fruit no good? but still good enough to eat round Christmas! (4–4)
7. Marl them about then mix a little oatmeal with water at the mouth of the sack! (8)
8. Scotland's largest national newsagents, tobacconists and confectioners, still retaining its founders initials and name (1,1,6)
13. Tent Wilson may have put up on the Lanarkshire-Peebleshire Border? (4,6)
15. Surname of Dunbartonshire-born novelist whose works include "Roderick Random" and "Peregrine Pickle" (8)
16. Darn over first man's bay on the Holy Loch! (8)
17. A well-known source of early potatoes, perhaps? (8)
19. Wood particles as a result of being bored sound as if they make a good fire! (6) . . .
20. . . . large burgh of Morayshire where the wood might be found by the sound of it! (6)
21. West coast shipcanal you will find in a load of fish! (6)

3

ACROSS

1. Want skill to become Scottish Reformation leader and martyr?(7)
5. Throw a little about the sheep no longer fit for breeding? (4,3)
9. "Ae fond kiss, and then we ——!
   Ae farewell, and then forever!" (Robert Burns: Ae fond kiss) (5)
10. Lothian Abbey about to start fresh fight? (9)
11. All ravens seem to enjoy consuming Scottish peas! (9)
12. Western Isle seen lying between Arrochar and Ranfurly Castle? (5)
13. Give up?—the sun is melting the frost! (5)
15. Grampian summit on which you can hang coral? (9)
18. Roman emperor who went to the Wall in Scotland ? (9)
19. Archbishop of York whose claim to ecclesiastical superiority over the Scots led to the Wars of Succession in the 15th & 16th Centuries (5)
21. Anger, we hear at getting duck in Lothians village? (5)
23. Very nearly the 'heavy' mobs whose ancestral home was once Wick Castle? (9)
25. Pearl mare transformed into the lamprey! (6–3)
26. Alive, and bailing water! (5)
27. Dried an assortment by thunder! (4–3)
28. The foundations of a haystack built with early Stewart and early Dawson! (7)

DOWN

1. Can our group err on an Orkney island? (7)
2. West Indian found in a street in Glasgow? (2,7)
3. Herdsman's summer residence sounds as if it's fine and open! (5)
4. Famous North Berwick castle, ancestral home of the Black Douglasses since 1370 (9)
5. A clown without end? – crazy goings-on at Argyllshire Highland Games? (5)
6. Bridge highest over border burgh? it's in Stirlingshire! (9)
7. Fester in Fettercairn? (5)
8. Better half of the 'Hammer of the Scots'? (7)
14. Dud land on Ayrshire coast? Well, the Stewarts enjoyed its castle! (9)
16. Sounds like Balmoral, Edinburgh, Stirling, etc., are all to be found around Maybole! (9)
17. Hal loving going around industrial area of Glasgow? (9)
18. A1 rider needs to negotiate Lanarkshire burgh? (7)
20. Sinless? Therefore get short 'release' from pain! (7)
22. The sharp-nosed eel is definitely less wild! (5)
23. Famous Glasgow cinema has poem about it, we read? (5)
24. Leash undone round the throat? (5)

4

ACROSS

1. Molar tooth has Miss Minelli turned upside-down! (4)
4. "Stern ruin's—share drives elate full on thy bloom" (Robert Burns: To a Mountain Daisy) (6)
9. Hebridean island colonized by S.W. area forms the most southerly part of the Scottish mainland! (4,2,8)
11. The longest highland sea-inlet on which you might find a witch? (4,5)
12. "—Catholic" Scots name for the Red Admiral Butterfly (5)
13. Reach with some difficulty—and organize? (6)
15. Tune caught in the midst of a clach—sung when doing housework badly! (8)
17. Winsome water in the middle of Perthshire? (4, 4)
18. Unseaworthy boat sounds as if it's divided up! (6)
21. Having knots in the head, we Scots hear (5)
22. A calm nell typifying Kircudbrightshire family whose seat was the now-ruined castle there? (9)
24. Novel by Neil M. Gunn relating to the highland clearances and its effects on the local fishing industry (6, 8)
25. Supercilious manner of the wattle of a turkey cock? (6)
26. Western sea-loch which sounds in good order! (4)

DOWN

2. A hundred bows, broken and requiring splint! (5)
3. Pull heavy weight to north Ayrshire village? (6)
4. A scrimmage sounds as if it's purple in a monopoly situation!(4-4)
5. "——cauld" song and poem written by Robert Burns (1,8)
6. Grassily amend a part of the Orkney group? (8,6)
7. What the thistle is to the Scots (6)
8. The more common Gaelic name for the mystical 'Stone of the Tubs' which sits at the foot of the town cross in Inverness (5-2-7)
10. Scottish island taking it on the chin? (4)
14. Tributary of the Spey—provider of raw material for malt whisky perhaps? (9)
16. Little village—a partner in one of Scotland's largest counties! (8)
17. Scottish loch shown in Tantallon Guide Books? (4)
19. Nationality of a King Canute, who was defeated by Scots King Malcolm III at the battle of Cruden Bay in 1012 (6)
20. A light slap for Scots means a bad shot in golf! (6)
23. The Spanish join Mr. Chaney in an Aberdeenshire village? (5)

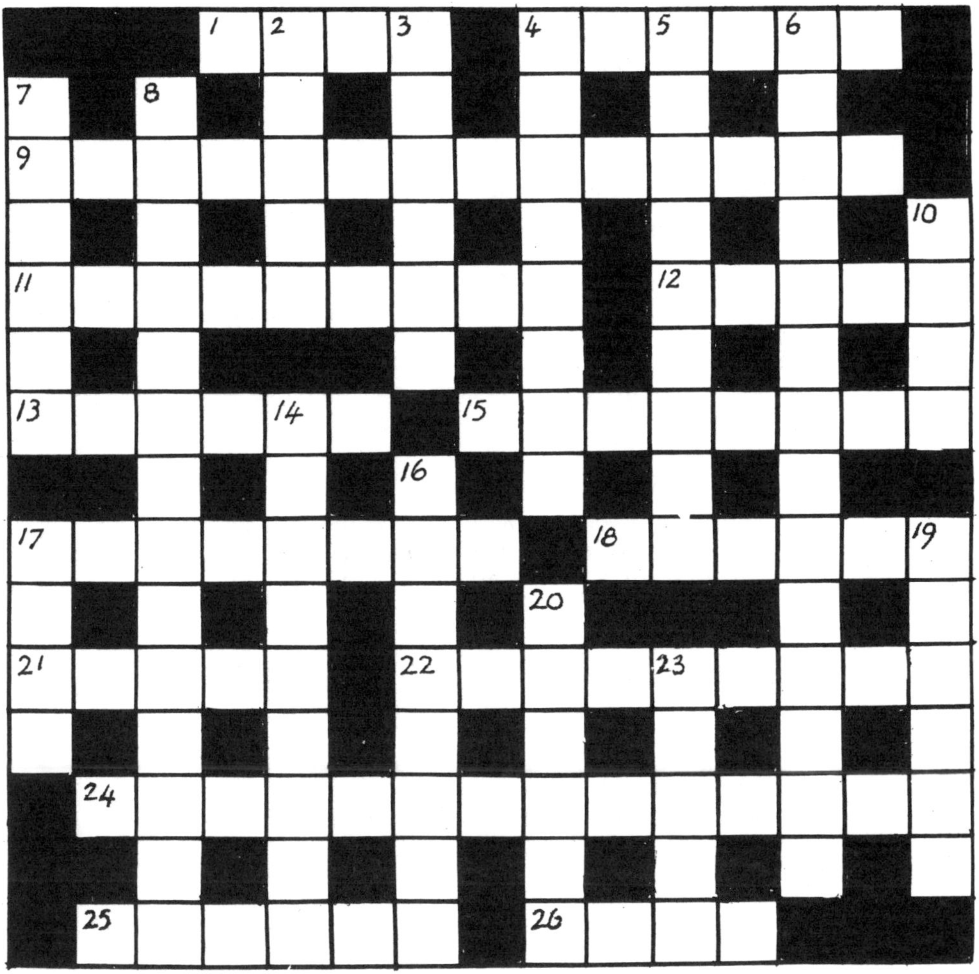

5

ACROSS

1. On which you will find a carefully measured mile? (5,2,5)
9. I ply Lovat turning in his golf swing perhaps? (9)
10. Dual learner's arrangement for the old Shetland law regarding the right of succession? (5)
11. Surname of the Kilmarnock-born clergyman who became Archbishop of Canterbury in 1980 (6)
12. Wode dog would paint on whisky starter and pottery? (8)
13. Scottish lady you might lose your head over! (6)
14. The honest and open land between Orkney and Sheltand? (4,4)
17. Senior Scottish Dukedom having a bit of a laugh at classic English poet? (8)
19. Rice pudding following more than once on ancient Stewarts hunting grounds round Perthshire burgh? (6)
21. The lady appears we hear — and ill becomes! (3–5)
23. Take snuff — and its result? (6)
25. A hundred left nothing right for a lazy, ill-dressed woman!(5)
26. Odd 'un? Land around 13th Century Ayrshire castle! (9)
27. Two Irishmen who between 1827 and 1828 were responsible for at least 15 deaths in Edinburgh, their victims bodies being sold to anatomists (5, 3, 4)

DOWN

2. Scottish doctrine preaching the nearness of the 2nd advent (9)
3. I lent it to the Scots meadow-pipit! (7)
4. Oil springing up from schoolyard? (4)
5. Shawfield Rules O.K.? O.K. on southern peak! (5,3)
6. Youthful Scottish Secretary of State? (7)
7. Muse from Ballater – a town for every tourist? (5)
8. Site of the Cheviot hills where, on Sept. 9th 1513, the Scots suffered their heaviest defeat at the hands of the English (7,5)
9. Hock mama mixed after another drink at the top of Tarbat Ness in Easter Ross? (12)
15. Distorted tune? Another indication of being drunk? (6,3)
16. Glasgow rail depot I made lop-sided? (8)
18. Trees the French make into a salmon spear? (7)
20. Managed without central heating on a Perthshire loch? (7)
22. Farm animal appears in broken antimony — requiring splint! (5)
24. What did you say? Border burgh losing heart? (4)

6

ACROSS

1. Sweet-nothing building standing near Hawick, seat of the earls of the same name? (5,5)
6. Brian Barnes' shot over a monstrous water hazard? (4)
10. Keep company with law returning to famous Argyllshire highland games site? (5)
11. Dunbartonshire village tune? Chord lost, though! (9)
12. See 7 down.
13. Greet worker on Ardnamurchan's highest peak? (5)
15. Um, train up to become Scottish long-distance and cross-country champion athlete? (3,4)
17. Plans originally laid at Foyers now extended throughout the highlands! (7)
19. It's unfair, being of different sizes! (7)
21. Small Celtic rowing boat made of skins stretched over a wicker frame (7)
22. Notary public with internal pay-back? — Snap! (5)
24. Hawick and Scotland rugby centre in Scotland's capital surrounded by two weights? (8)
27. Tweed tributary often short? (5,4)
28. Champion Gaelic boy? (5)
29. Peak near Golspie, – it could be a hoot! (4)
30. Scottish politician who founded the Independent Labour Party in the 19th century (4,6)

DOWN

1. Name given to fertilizer on the inner Hebridean Isle? (4)
2. Table went about site of Abbey near Dalkeith? (9)
3. Apply lubrication — and flatter? (3, 2)
4. Village of Aberdeenshire, sounds like just the place to send mother! (3,4)
5. "—questions" Church of Scotland idiom for the shorter catechism without proof texts (7)

7,12. Scottish singer whose most famous work is her rendition of "The Old Rugged Cross" (5, 8)

8. Reel name of a great highland valley? (10)
9. Watery creation of 17 across–sounds as if its an extension!(4,4)
14. Parliamentary constituency which will take more than guns or something to win? (5, 5)
16. "Lay the proud —— low"(Robert Burns: Scots Wha Hae) (8)
18. Surname of the Lossiemouth-born politician who became British P.M. in 1924 (9)
20. Large north-west sea inlet, — doubling as sheep-dip? (4,3)
21. Can R.N. teach us how to play the bagpipes in part? (7)
23. Old nag which I confuse with Vera? (5)
25. Western point of Argyllshire lying somewhere between Ardrossan and Nairn? (5)
26. Scots Black and Blue? Lay the blame on the loss of a thousand! (4)

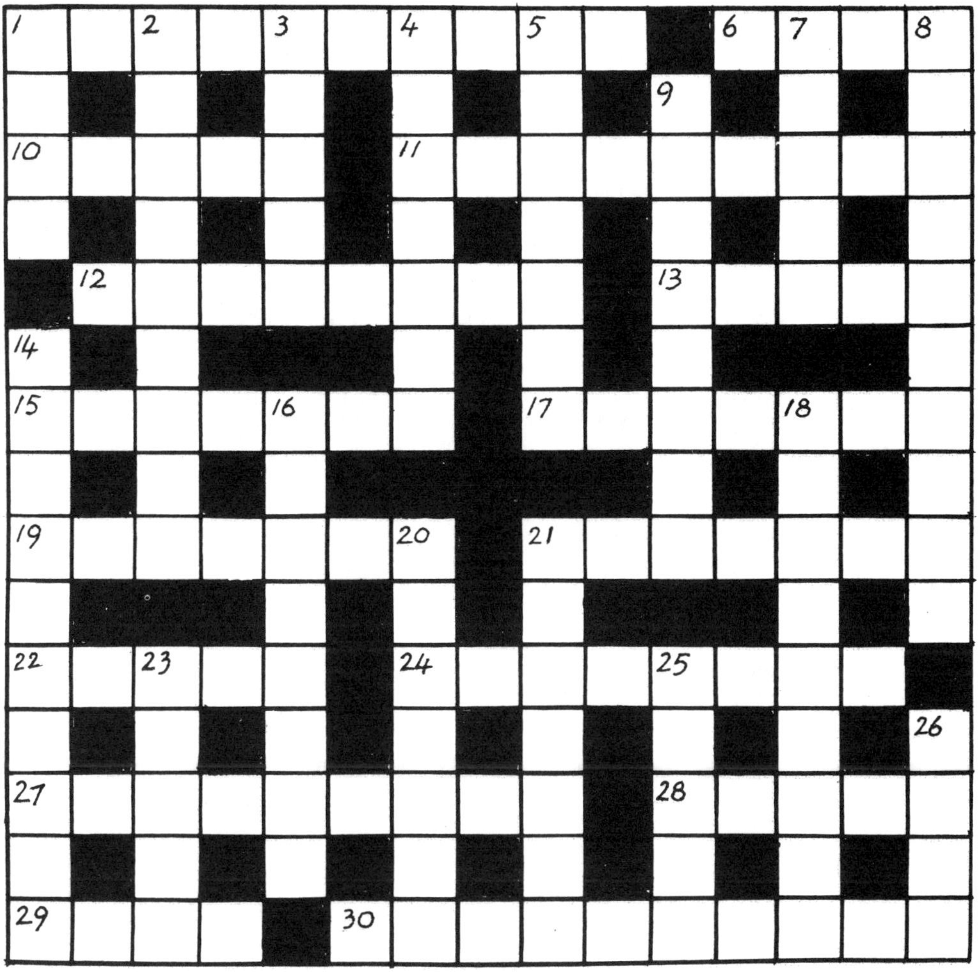
1
2
3
4
5
6
7
8
9
10
11
12
13
14
15
16
17
18
19
20
21
22
23
24
25
26
27
28
29
30

7

ACROSS

1. Scots inventor who designed the first steamboat to ply on any river in Europe, the 'Comet' in 1812 (5,4)
8. A French and an English article preceding puddle in Sutherland hamlet? (7)
9. Oil platforms not working? — or just the dresses worn there ! (7)
10. Beat Ray about having caught him in dangerous sandbank off Buddonness near Carnoustie? (7)
13. "— — — thought, my youthfu' friend"
(Robert Burns: Epistle to a Young Friend) (1,4,3)
14. Talk at length about a quantity of paper? (4)
16. Historic castle situated about 4 miles S.E. of Alloa used as Police Training College. (10)
20. Strong grass seen in Pitsligo skiing holiday? (4) ...
22. ... Rye with grassy top arranged to reveal a powerful, malignant spirit! (4)
24. Decries tin mined in a religious area? (10)
28. Alastair Milne's medium for broadcasting to Loch in Shetland! (4)
29. With broken rear jaw point to a punter! (8)
31. Ane grab — enough to capture military company? (7)
34. And French meant to upset annuity scheme? (7)
35. Surname of the famous Scots portrait painter who died in 1823, aged 67 (7)
36. National emblems resulting from a push to the French? (9)

DOWN

1. See 30.
2. Ian Lang — a disorderly man with a bunion? (3-4)
3. Early with fireworks but no Guy? (5)
4. Laws Lee breaks, as usual! (7)
5. "And in the vats of — this year the must shall foam"
(Macauley: Lays of Ancient Rome) (4)
6. Sparrow used to encourage horse? (4)
7. The harvest-home made of hard earth and rock mostly! (7)
11. See 22 down.
12.& 25. Famous poem by Burns whose first line is "When Chapman Billies leave the street," (3,1,7)
15. Against having a drink? (4)
17. Hazy about Crookfur youth centre? (37
18. Unravel Scottish snowball manufacturers? (4)
19. Liar leaves Ailsa Craig and gets transport to Sutherland Loch! (6)
21. Implement much in evidence on the foot of Glenshee! (3)
22.& 11. Scots Churchman and historian who wrote "History of My Own Times". He died in 1715, aged 72. (7,6)
23. Make lion noise — that's uncommon by the sound of it! (4)
25. See 12.
26. More rye-grass mown by Lord Len? (7)
27. With reds out on all sides, ran to get the shopping? (7)
30.& 1. down. Scots vet and author, his life story provided the theme for B.B.C.TV's successful series "All Creatures Great and Small" (5,7)
32. Scottish mountain returning to Burnmouth — well, the tip of it, anyway! (4)
33. The emphasis has to be put on crazy young teenager! (4)

8

ACROSS

3. I told him an awful thing about a Scottish county? (10)
8. Sounds like romantic southern continent might contain water in Inverness-shire? (6)
9. Initially cuts up Scottish labour federation? (4)
10. Ayrshire town where the big bunnets come from? (10)
11. "—— Collinwood" It's Scots for the four of hearts! (3)
13. & 25. R.P.M.? National arrangement for Scots symbol! (4,7)
14. Labourer seen around Banffshire town? (8)
16. Anne around looking for no-one? (4)
18. Banal form of the ancient Pictish kingdom? (5)
21. Chimney loses you formerly in order to cross it to the Hebrides? (5)
23. Spoil, we hear, Troon college? (4)
26. S.M. in Alva? No – the Argentinian Falklands! (8)
27. Thin river flowing through Dumfries? (4)
28. Account gets article – gets drive! (3)
29. She was bonnie to Burns, Streep out to get Holywood actress – wife of Howard Hughes! (4,6)
30. "Ev'n —— who mourn'st the daisy's fate," (Burns: To A Mountain Daisy) (4)
31. Colin about to add learner to class held by Strathclyde professor who with Sir Wm. Lithgow, produced a plan for Scottish shipbuilding called 'Oceanspan'! (6)
32. The governing body of Scotland first held in Scone by King Kenneth III in 838 A.D. (10)

DOWN

1. & 27. In Scots law, advertisement required for any process to continue e.g. the building of a house, etc. (8,6)
2. People not needing wet-suits near Loch Lomond? (6)
3. Cam ring needed to make Scotland's 1982 world cup captain go? (7)
4. Doon arrangment – vehicle for 1960's Scots balladeer? (7)
5. Russian seaport using Caledonian Canal ferry boat! (4)
6. Move forward and complain about island in Loch Lomond? (4,4)
7. Modern town situated on River Tay? Not quite! (8)
12. Back Gaelic, but can be beaten! (4)
15. Carry a stone for husking barley? (4)
17. Egyptian dancing girl from Dalmarnock? (4)
18. Formerly a 'training' ground in Dundonald? (Ayrshire) (4,4)
19. Football? A terrible thing in beautiful Aberdeenshire town! (8)
20. Go up the Nile? – He's the very devil! (4)
22. Small bed and early trellis make up vice-chancellor of Stirling University! (8)
24. At St. Rae? – No it's a goddess of power! (7)
25. See 13 across
27. See 1 down
29. Indian rule over Uist capital? Move away to another island? (4)

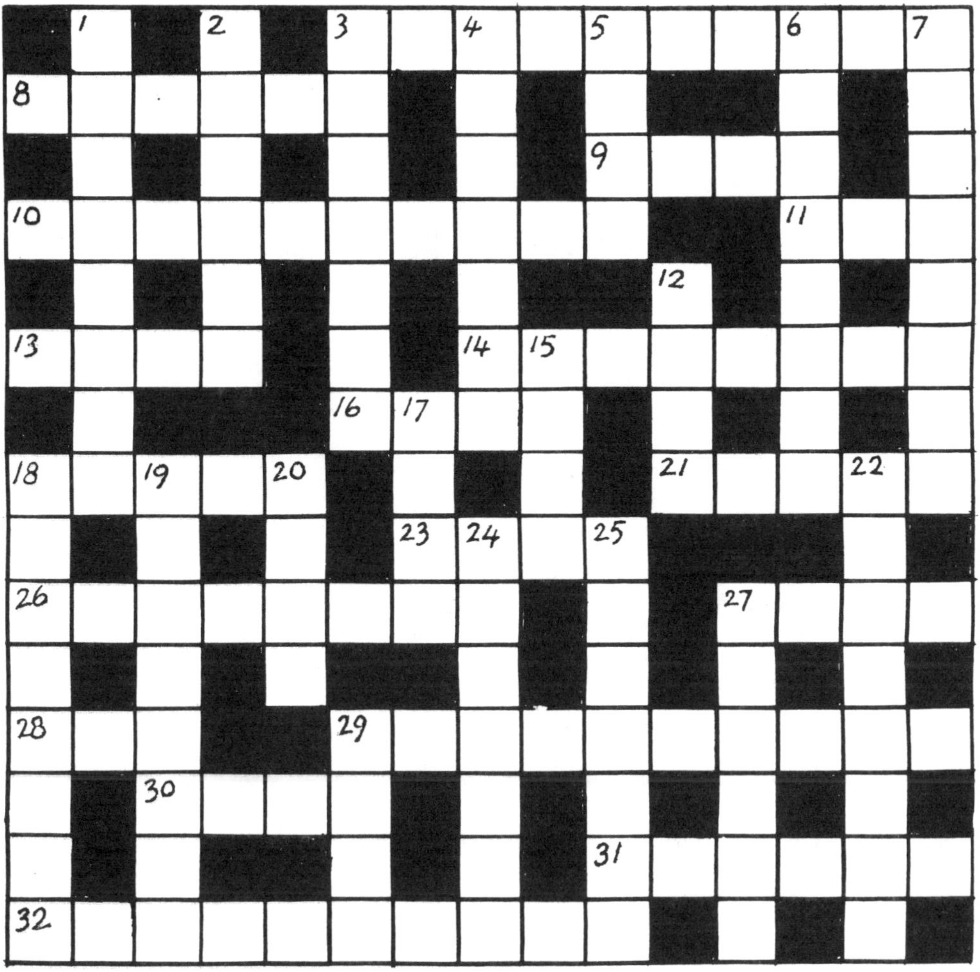

1
2
3
4
5
6
7
8
9
10
11
12
13
14
15
16
17
18
19
20
21
22
23
24
25
26
27
28
29
30
31
32

9

ACROSS

1. Soapy bit thrown at a soldier? (7)
5. Her cats stagger about! (7)
9. North Scottish county whose main town is Dingwall (4,3,8)
10. What is the object? A hat-tassel! (6)
12. Let oil out for 20th century Scots politician and associate of J.M. Bridie? (6)
13. Is inside a German house-eaves! (5)
15. "——The Horn" Scots expression for a year of life (4,2)
16. Grade 'R'—all right for a day-labourer? (6)
17. Unfar?—Nonsense you're nearly drunk! (3,2)
18. I am Eck!—What a way to introduce a rector of Dundee University! (6)
19. Inner 'E'?—It puts the 'R' in Mackintosh designer! (6)
21. Apt name for peer and former Scots' Secretary of State? (5)
22. Family who first ruled Scotland in 1371 and maintained a claim to the British throne until 1807 (6)
24. Sacs up? Makes beds for oysters! (6)
28. Mary Queen of Scots prison until her 'escape' to England in 1567 (9,6)
29. Lum up—Ayrshire river makes up famous Scottish racehorse owner! (7)
30. Loch Nay? No place for the kingfisher! (7)

DOWN

1. Tar nets up, then have a good hearty meal! (7)
2. Since 1974 the name given to a local government body (8,7)
3. Can one door be used as a multi-coloured marble? (5)
4. Make a date with a sheep-louse? (4)
5. South or North? that's the decision to be made to reach Ayrshire village! (4)
6. Lam me with moving part of flail which hits grain? (5)
7. Is this board in opposition to the Scots white-fish authority? (7,8)
8. Rob's mate starts off being a bully (7)
11. Scottish lager brewer only on a lease? (7)
12. Ure returns to Dens—about and lasts! (7)
14. Can a bush really hide a mean, grasping person? (5)
18. Lamlash involved with small swop? as far as grain is concerned it's a right mix-up! (7)
20. Before 1948 part of fast-moving sign between King's Cross and Waverley! (7)
23. Piece of bread has nothing for the Scottish earldom created in 1651! (5)
25. Credit, being unwell in Fifeshire town? (5)
26. Bravo, Ninians place is flowing through Stirlingshire! (4)
27. Can the Minches conceal Scottish Island? (4)

10

ACROSS

1. Hae story about "The Madeira of Scotland"? (8)
5. Liquifies steel and makes smooth spots on the sea? (6)
9. Bag at the Lothians industrial town? (8)
10. Rep, Len has to convince is more abundant? (6)
12. I pop up in sick troop – we're all hoarse! (6)
13. Castle lying 2 miles north of Kilmarnock, birth place of Elizabeth Mure – 'mother' of the Stewart line of kings (8)
15. Goes white about little bell sound and radio enthusiast—repairs to Lothian home of former Prime Minister A.J. Balfour! (12)
18. Peebleshire town popularised by Sir Walter Scott who used it as the scene of his novel "St. Ronan's Well" (12)
23. Draw for Clyde initially? playing against Lanarkshire village side! (8)
24. Urr? — sue about interest charger? (6)
26. Let tap flow with spade used for cleaning plough? (6)
27. Punctuation mark? – speak about it on fertile part of Inner Hebrides! (8)
28. Standing up – Reseat specially? (6)
29. Scottish burgh where football is played on the links! (8)

DOWN

1. The common factor of Bruce and Burns? (6)
2. Skin drawing done in Edinburgh only during August? (6)
3. "The —— Bible, a book which, if everything else in our language should perish, would alone suffice to show the whole extent of its beauty and power." (Macauley: On John Dryden — Edinburgh Review of Jan. 1828) (7)
4. It's a way of saying 'oats'! (4)
6. Mail gal delivers visiting major fishing port? (7)
7. Learner with race comes towards farm animal with chain (6,2)
8. "The untented Kosmos my abode, I pass, a wilful ——" (R.L. Stevenson: Songs of Travel) (8)
11. Sip pots made up for Roman Catholics? (7)
14. Sweetheart loses sugar – preposition added substantially? (2,5)
16. Pale Pict seen in distress round village to the north of Inverurie? (8)
17. Traces an old Scots earldom whose seat is at Muthill, near Crieff? (8)
19. Insurrections found on ladies' dresses perhaps? (7)
20. Shore? It is found on Skye sea-loch! (7)
21. The quick part of Prestonpans? (6)
22. Famous Glasgow street sounds as though it must run north-west! (6)
25. Mint favoured by the Duke of Rothesay? (4)

1 2 3 4 5 6 7 8
9 10
11
12 13
14
15
16 17
18 19 20
21 22
23 24
25
26 27
28 29

11

ACROSS

1, 20 Popular name given to the leader of the Jacobite movement in 1745 (6,6,7)
9. Crown about upsetting rate of grain payment made by farmers to pay for the upkeep of a mill? (5-4)
10. "—— —— The North" popular title given to the Dukes of Gordon (4,1)
11. In getting strange grin after displacing the 'shot' in curling? (6)
12. Ancient Scottish family who own most of the Isle of Islay (8)
13. Dual return to Queen giving Scottish music hall entertainer of the early 20th Century! (6)
14. Hitch men find when crossing to the Hebrides? (3,5)
17. Does it always need a foreman to use spring shears on sheep? (8)
19. The name on many a Scottish export! (6)
21. Where the standard should be in Angus village? (8)
23. Judges hammer, we hear, – requirement for living riotously! (6)
25. In the main, a showing of what a man can mow a day? (5)
26. 20th century Scots author whose works include "Laxdale Hall" and "Private Angelo" (9)
27. Like Loch Venn? – one might expect to find it 21 miles south of Fort William? (12)

DOWN

2. Northumberland village giving Scots a 1388 victory! (9)
3. Northern Ireland in firing line? – only if orange! (7)
4. Enough for Burns? (4)
5. Yon ranch looks as though it's covered with bracken! (8)
6. N.E. march about in search of horse-leather! (7)
7. Seek about a hundred and adds to! (5)
8. N.Cloch?—errand has to be run to grain merchant? (4-8)
9. Flourishes by circulation teeth-holders? (12)
15. Ben Wattle becomes subject to earthquake, rebuilt as historic Midlothian Abbey! (9)
16. The golfers 'fore'! of dirty water? (8)
18. Sun sins over a tiny amount? (7)
20. See 1
22. Ark – it may wander idly to and fro! (5)
24. Part of foot found on Scottish island? (4)

1
2
3
4
5
6
7
8
9
10
11
12
13
14
15
16
17
18
19
20
21
22
23
24
25
26
27

12

ACROSS

1. See 17
6. Cads about fisherman's ray? (4)
10. Touring around lowing like a cow? (7)
11. "—— fish" Scots expression for the narwhal, because of its appearance (7)
12. Stir camel up for old Scots clan? (9)
13. Farm servant always at the back, we hear? (5)
14. Painted ceramic marble – a favourite out East? (5)
15,7. Distinction last gained by Scotland's rugby team in 1984 (3,6,5)
17,1,22. Famous line from the first verse of Burns' poem "Is there for honest poverty" (4,2,3,3,7,5)
20. Stay about the east and become successful Edinburgh-born 19th century editor and playwright! (5)
21. Welles important to Macbeth in the early 1950's? (5)
23. Scottish Knight who was Mary, Queen of Scots, regent (4,5)
25. Brae is a roundabout way of describing a maligner! (7)
26. Long-winded way of saying 'inconclusive'? (7)
27. Washes sheep – and ducks? (4)
28. Covering card game in Lanarkshire? (10)

DOWN

1. Hurt upset Malcolm initially, being at a loose-end? (5)
2. School subject of John Knox's 1560 book "First Book of Discipline"! (9)
3. Movement, popular during Burns' time, and to which he subscribed, which found the basis of moral distinction in the use of actions (14)
4. "—— - ——-eenie" children's final playtime before going to bed (5, 2)
5. Lure Mae out to remote Perthshire village between the Tay and the Almond? (7)
7. See 15
8. Render sad dishevelled strollers? (9)
9. Scottish knight and composer whose works included "I love a Lassie" and "Roamin' in the Gloamin"! (3,5,6)
14. Do a clan? Dr. must set up practice in part of Glasgow! (9)
16. Aped thereabouts Aberdeenshire fishing port? (9)
18. Water remover has a little number going in Midlothian, perhaps? (7)
19. Pitch Robert partly deals with on Harris? (7)
22. See 17
24. Son is backward? that is as plain as the nose on his face! (5)

SCAD
CROWN
THETRIPLE
PEPPERHEAD
SINOS

13

ACROSS

1. Scottish Football team manager during 1982 world cup finals (4,5)
6. Wiles about the largest of the Hebrides? (5)
9. Sounds like you have faith in a meeting place! (5)
10. Economist, peer and author whose works include "The Earnings Conflict" and "Piecework Abandoned" (4,5)
11. Two saints about flat on Ayrshire coastal burgh? (10)
12. Famous salmon river rising in the Grampian mountains and reaching the Moray Firth at Kingston (4)
14. Feather pen on the cross-guard of a Scots sword handle? (7)
15. Former American President who founded St. Salvator's College, St. Andrews in 1450? (7)
17. Could she be called "The Hammer of the Scots wife"? (7)
19. "I will —— her until you hear the pips squeak" (Sir Eric Geddes: World War I address on Germany) (7)
20. An indefinite number – ten out against! (4)
22. They set try in order – what nonsense! (5–5)
25. The other half of Scottish Breweries? (9)
26. Shout Ole! at resignation of an annual rent? (5)
27. All are hungry? (5)
28. Scottish cricket extras? well in that direction anyway (5,4)

DOWN

1. Dundee exports to European race? (5)
2. Indefinite geographical area around Glasgow stretching westwards (9)
3. Hand lustre seen in Northern Scotland? (10)
4. Soil Len over a shoemakers tool? (7)
5. Family title of Thomas Howard, 3rd duke, who led the English forces at Flodden (7)
6. Boil over a Renfrewshire loch? (4)
7. Can hide and seek also be a symptom of dangerous cough? (5)
8. Young Scots golfer who has compiled the Dunlop Guide to Scottish Courses (5,4)
13. Scotland's Solicitor General was M.P. for this constituency in 1982 (5,5)
14. Last of the Stuarts who was first in furniture, perhaps? (5,4)
16. "The business of —— is the business of nobody" (Lord Macauley: Historical essay contributed to the Edinburgh Review) (9)
18. Story about a certain part of Glasgow? (7)
19. See byre and then strain ale? (3,4)
21. Cattle in the old days could sound like nothing on earth? (5)
23. Odds against suggests suitable mate? (5)
24. Scottish Queen who became monarch in 1542 when only one week old (4)

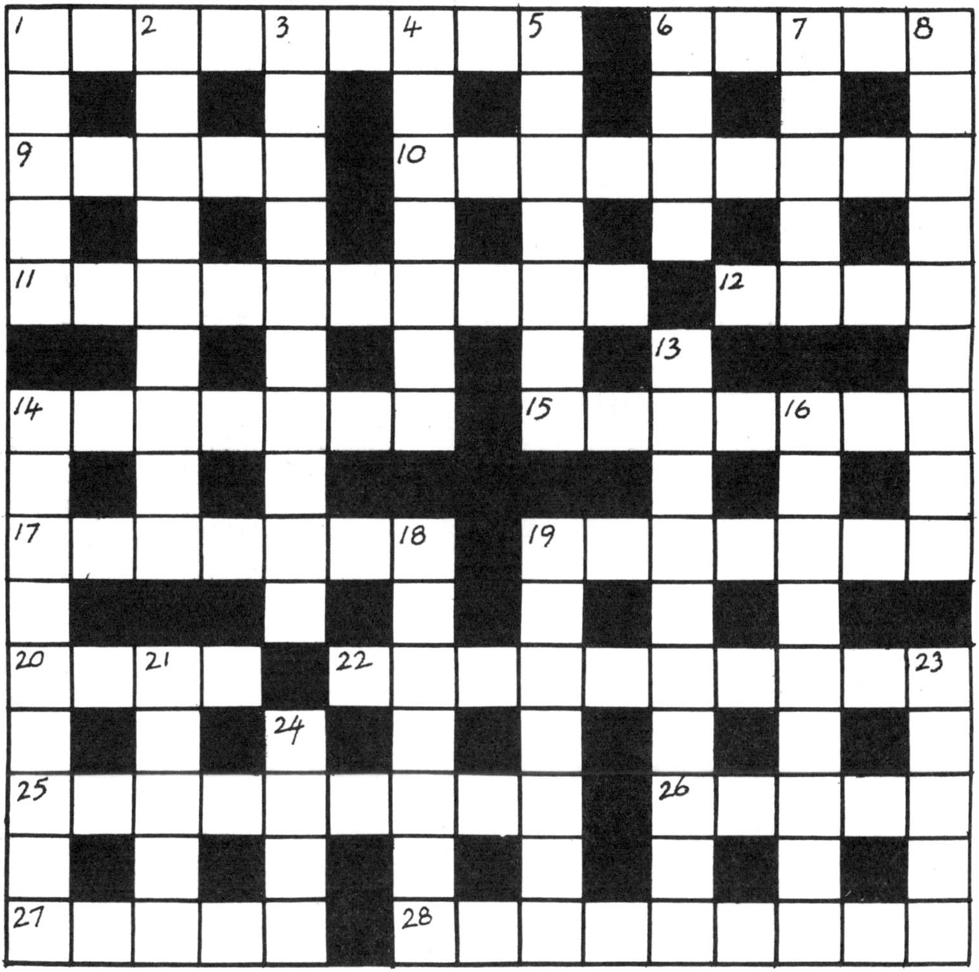

14

ACROSS

1. Lanarkshire burgh where there is a distinct lack of rain by the sound of it? (7)
5. Furnish with a drink for Aberdeenshire farming area! (7)
9,12. Scottish striker playing for Liverpool F.C. in 1980's (5, 8)
10. Carron – ITC Union? name of several Scots villages (9)
11. Union of crowns-head announced by Papal messenger? (6)
12. See 9
14. Circle destroys tank and makes a fuss! (5)
15. Kyle about riser being 'watcher' of the dead prior to burial! (4-5)
18. Surname of 18th Century Gaelic Poet famous for his pictorial descriptions of the highlands (9)
20. Down a point? sorted out and talked foolishly? (5)
22. Scots author, born in Cambusnethan, Lanarkshire, whose works include "Valerus" and "Adam Blair" (8)
24. Little early biscuit – it's the ragwort! (6)
26. Rose gaily swings about on chandelier? (9)
27. Can a potato sound partly like a trumpet to a Scots child? (5)
28. Chorale arrangment one of four strung along the Lunan Burn fault in Perthshire? (3–4)
29. Rakes about, that is to say 'restive'! (7)

DOWN

1. 1452 battle near the River Esk where King James II defeated the Earl of Douglas (9)
2. No trunk can be tied by sailors? (3-4)
3. Oy! Katrine – provide Glasgow Celtic with central defender (3, 6)
4. Win a Perthshire loch? (4)
5. Famous steeplechaser adds table-top to become sandwiched between Lomond and Katrine! (4,6)
6. Angry way to jeer? (5)
7. Bad start, clock sound has musty old grain? (7)
8. A thousand? small distance between the Hebrides and mainland! (5)
13. Chas. Reilly — maker of liquorice? (10)
16. Erse, a twin cannot understand, being restless? (9)
17. Sir, weeder is to be found in border settlement! (9)
19. Looks up, only having one spot left at dominoes? (5,2)
21. "Willie was a —— guid, could stown a clue wi' onie bodie" (Robert Burns: Willie Wastle) (7)
22. Scots ear with argon mined at Ayrshire pit village? (5)
23. "Thou, —— —— a' diseases" (Robert Burns: Address to the Toothache) (4,1)
25. Dahomey and Bahamas combine to make Scots pools? (4)

15

ACROSS

1. Money measure seen as old Celtic church site on the eastern shore of Loch Lomond? (7)
5. Hunting jet running Scotland's burghs? (7)
9. Tavern from within Eskdale? (5)
10. Rest around crabs in Caithness village? (9)
11. Pain Queen has to undergo to solve Logarithms inventor? (6)
12. Prized, and very rare, part of rhino nearly found on the Solway Firth? (8)
14. Fife loch starts, after the birth of Christ, to create water nymph! (5)
15. Coil three might find in Ayrshire village? (9)
18. Rob Roy was one! (9)
20. Church of England in the red? – that deserves a lecture! (5)
22. R. E. man Tam had a weapon! (8)
24. Scots family to lay great store by, perhaps? (6)
26. Rarer ants seen going to Ireland from here? (9)
27. Surname of the Scots boxer who was British Featherweight Champion in the early 1960's (5)
28. Can horn be arranged near Perthshire loch? (7)
29. Wander about aimlessly with piece of circus equipment? (7)

DOWN

1. Would you credit roaming about can produce famous Scots peak? (9)
2. Dens P. – A1 for beach construction? (4–3)
3. Description ideal for Dunfermline Athletic footballer? – only if he's poor! (9)
4. Surplus scotch yielding picturesque Loch Lomondside village? (4)
5. Goes in Parliament with Kinross and West! (10)
6. Two ducks with a morsel? a hairy caterpillar! (5)
7. Grue too much for moving tenant? (7)
8. Then – right in the middle of a ghost story (5) . . .
13. . . . ghoul returns to Ghana, nae wonder with U.K.'s largest lake! (5,5)
16. Arran's most northerly village once popular on Ayr racecourse? (9)
17. Renfrewshire burgh, reputed birthplace of the Scots outlaw Sir William Wallace (9)
19. Dr. Finlay partner – A.M. Crone! (7)
21. Before human tissue inside could give lowest bridging point of the Clyde? (7)
22. Rears someone who always backs out of a promise? (5)
23. Any Scottish mountain over 3,000 ft. named after the man who made an original list of them. (5)
25. Wart slots turn inside out and finished with – wart? (4)

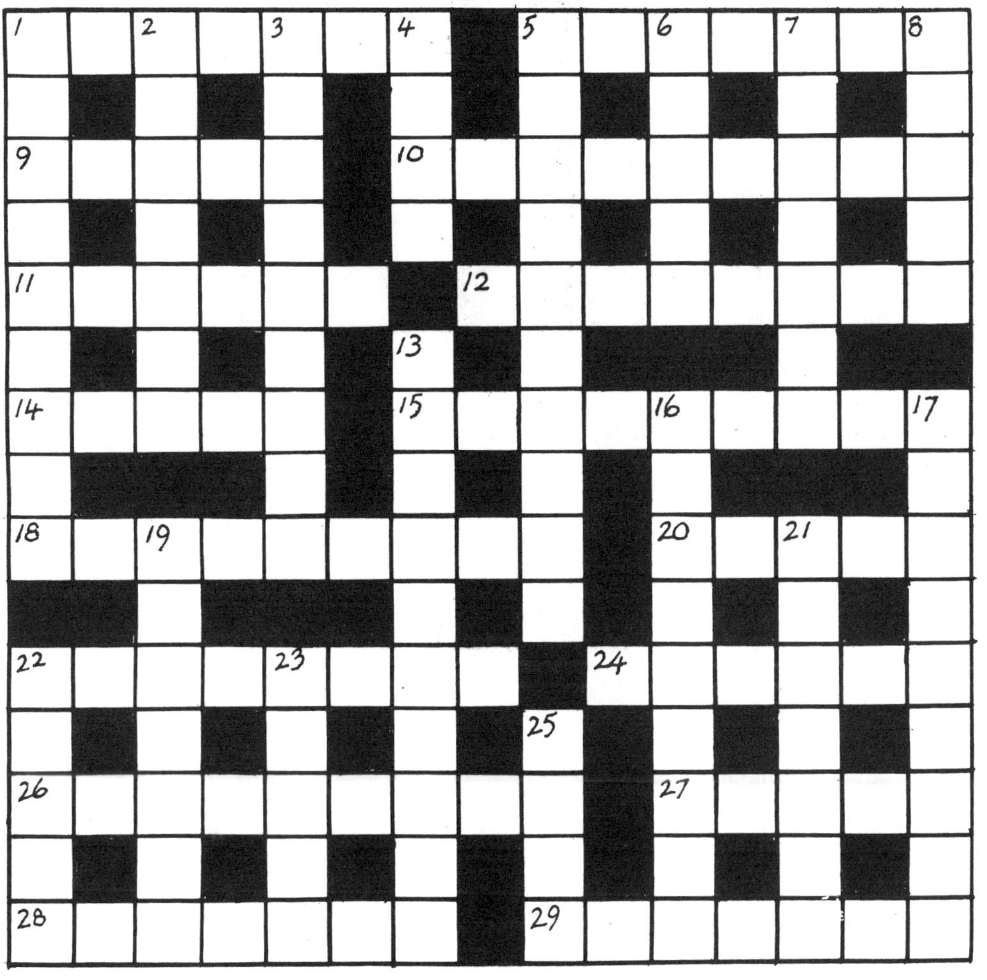

16

ACROSS

1. French Princess who just 40 days after marrying James V, died aged sixteen (9)
6. Big person found in little street with lamb's father? (5)
9. Old ruin as an incentive to piety in the Roman Catholic faith? (5)
10. Tam, magic about right to speak proper? (9)
11. It's true! in Scots law, land, trees, minerals etc.! (4, 6)
12. Hebridean name – the North, outer; the South, inner! (4)
14. Record early Hebridean has of us and young citizen of ancient Greece? (7)
15. Contemporary church found in the Dee valley between Ballater and Huntly? (7)

17, 2. Scots-born professional golfer whose club is Wentworth Surrey (7, 9)

19. "For the gay beams of lightsome day gild, but to flout ——— ———s grey" (Sir Walter Scott: Lay of the Last Minstrel) (3, 4)
20. Look closely at obtaining Royal burgh situated on the Dornoch Firth? (4)
22. Irish village port – the closest to Scotland, being only 21½ miles away (10)
25. Farm animal hesitates before adding weight to Gretna's old rival for the under 21's! (9)
26. Sailors behind seen on tributary of River Ayr? (5)
27. Old comic-hero gets right into Scots challenger! (5)
28. Elizabeth I's older sister and ally of the Queen of Scots (4,5)

DOWN

1. Roam about Robert initially and become Scotland's deepest loch! (5)
2. See 17.
3. Beach a lune must sort out in Aberdeenshire village? (10)
4. Stranraer – Gateshead route followed by worker ant? (7)
5. Welshman carrying weight? only as far as a village, east of Dingwall! (7)
6. Yes, minehead arrangement can give Scottish surgeon who invented a form of amputation! (4)
7. Rodent with little house in conservation area of Midlothian? (9)
8. Hundred men about break can give old Scots family name! (9)
13. Abbey near Criffel, Dumfriesshire, founded in 1275 – for lovers only perhaps? (10)
14. Under pressure such as med. around Bannockburn for example? (9)
16. At Dunedin and completely overwhelmed? (9)
18. Circle saint found in dram? luckily, one of Columba's pupils! (7)
19. Scots meddler, looking after football squad? (7)
21. German always becomes a Scottish bird! (5)
23. Two points repeatedly right, it's inferior! (5)
24. Abbey near Peterhead – a source of venison? (4)

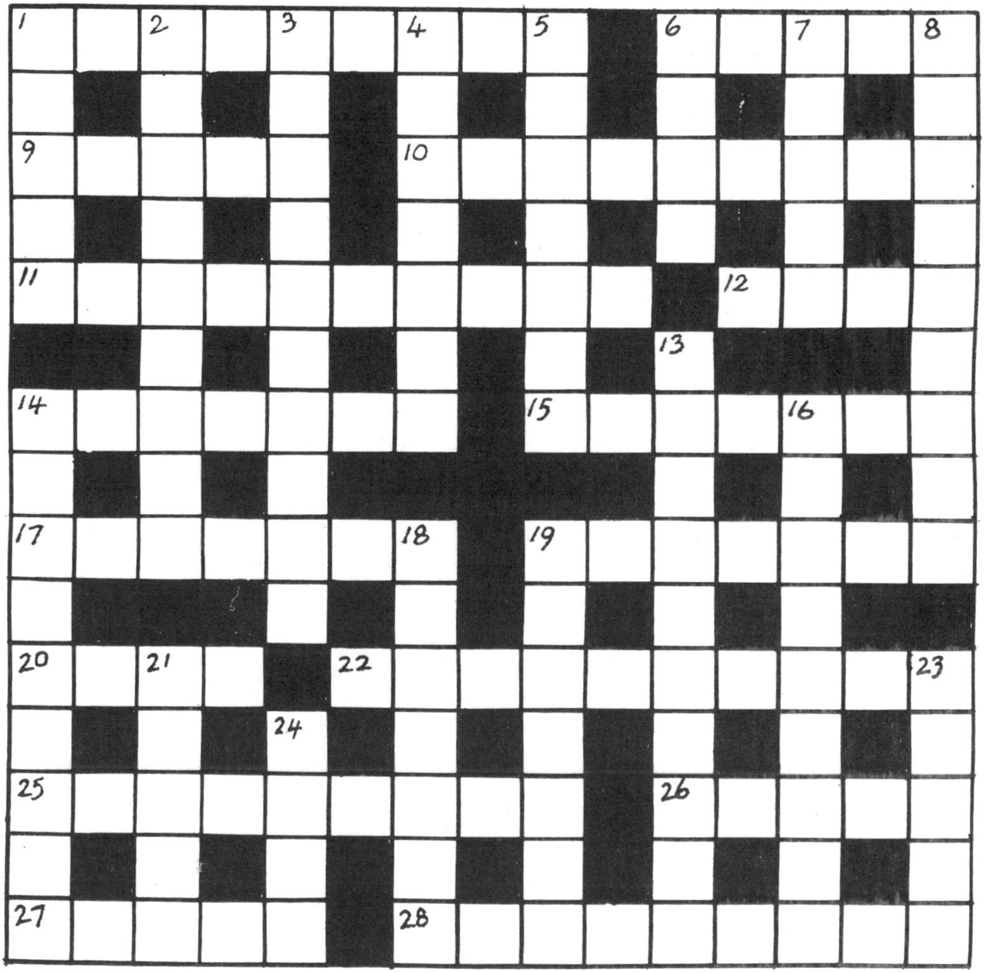
1
2
3
4
5
6
7
8
9
10
11
12
13
14
15
16
17
18
19
20
21
22
23
24
25
26
27
28

17

ACROSS

1. See 11.
4. Writer whose sole subject is the crab-apple? (6)
8. Title of R. L. Stevenson's last (and unfinished) novel (4, 2, 9)
10. Bruce's Boy? Queen's physician in Scotland since 1977! (9)
11, 1. Aston Villa and Scotland defender who played in the 1982 World Cup (5, 5)
12. Scottish shipbuilding plant? (6)
14. Ross is mad about crit lying on writing-desks? (8)
16. Old Scots family name roughly translated as 'son of Glengarry' that is! (8)
17. Fins return the French bridle? (6)
20. Runner with nothing on the children's comic of yesterday! (5)
21. After the Spanish reds lie about burgh near Paisley! (9)
23. The common policy of Keir Hardie? (15)
24. Hangman's rope from tritium and chemical liquid? (6)
25. Kite and Hawk's head combine and become delicate? (5)

DOWN

1. Place to look up to in Scotland's capital! (9, 6)
2. First journey across? (5)
3. Scot loses nothing inserting his type of rock! (6)
4. Scorn Che? upset he makes a shrill cry! (8)
5. Union rat I dismember resulting from over-use of alcohol, perhaps? (9)
6. One spelt defeat in 1298 for Sir William Wallace, the other a victory for the Jacobites in 1746 (6, 2, 7)
7. Oy! Brew up over there! (6)
9. Sane member about for the time being! (5)
13. Stoor got round to hospital? old Europeans will fix it! (9)
15. Robert Burns 'Twa Brigs' fought over it, perhaps? (5, 3)
16. My good French former M.P. for Greenock? (5)
18. The last word on Macbeth! (6)
19. In Scots law, deliberate with a view to a judgement – and save about five hundred and one? (6)
22. A quarter of a year with broken heart? (5)

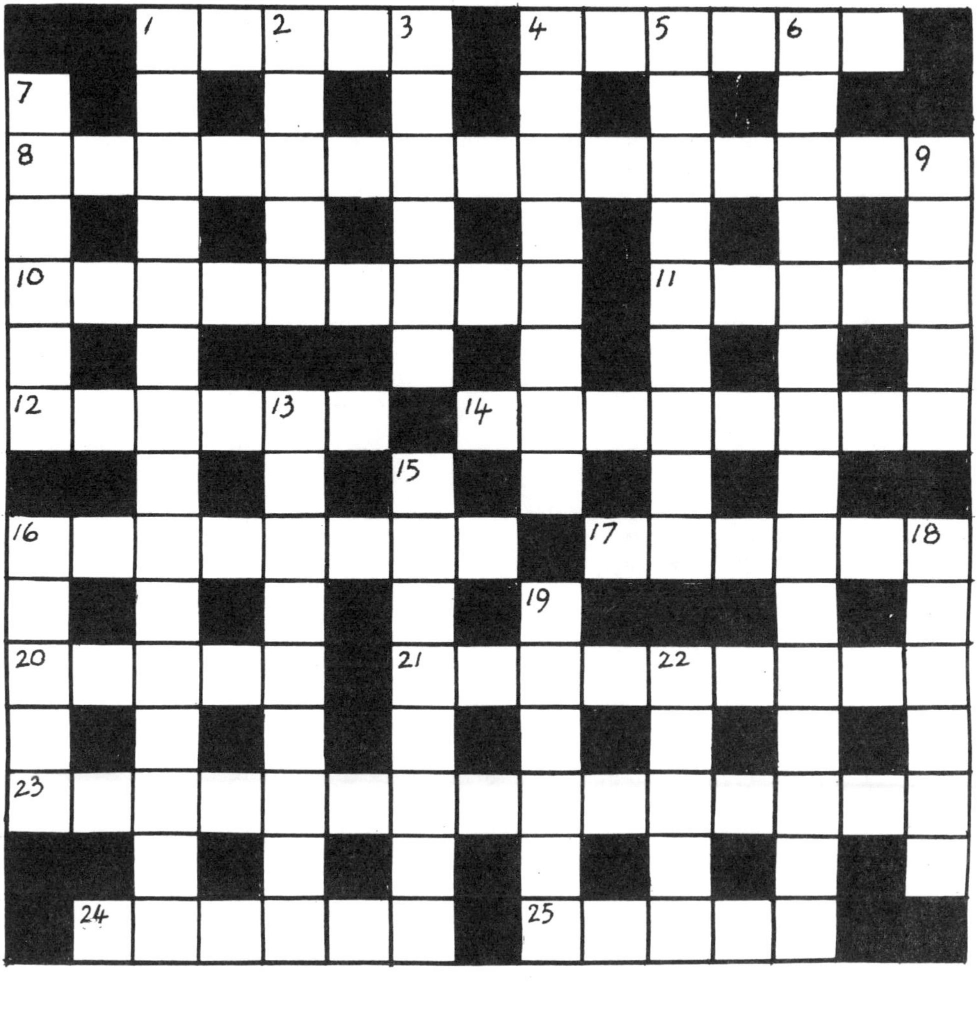
1
2
3
4
5
6
7
8
9
10
11
12
13
14
15
16
17
18
19
20
21
22
23
24
25

18

ACROSS

1. I long with fifty otherwise in West Lothian burgh! (10)
6. See 14.
10. Fish wife takes in learner who eats very quickly! (7)
11. Bank return is easy initially for a short, stout person! (7)
12. A kiss around Cleo? she's just a young girl! (9) . . .
13. . . . if she's black she often goes to prison! (5)

14, 6. Famous Orkney naval base, which after World War I was designated a national war grave (5, 4)

15. I get grass – growing wild about border village! (9)
17. Highlander's cap which should only be found in the valley of Mr. Owen? (9)
20. Be happy to come from Netherlee set? (5)
21. Niger recolonised? go about beating a drum! (5)
23. County town after drinking establishment? You'll find it in east Glasgow park (9)
25. Sheep dip largely found in Ross and Cromarty? (4, 3)
26. Starling loses tail – settles again for bodily interiors! (7)
27. Saffron loses shout and winds up on Shetland isle! (4)
28. Her great S.S. man is drunk and tottering with others! (10)

DOWN

1. Lawful time allowed before foreclosure of a mortgage? (5)
2. Lady's cloak named after Dumfriesshire countess who hid her husband in one when assisting him in escaping from the Tower of London (9)
3. Part of Wales whose people singularly, have a culture identical to that of Lothians and Galloway (4,2,8)
4. Elk hair about to become animals pelt! (7)
5. Rone sky seen over North of Scotland? (7)
7. Reels composed especially for a wrong-doer? (5)
8. Old Scots curse? – sounds like a question about a tail! (3, 4, 2)
9. Deeside retreat fit for a king! (8, 6)
14. Do you have to have a sweet friend to share liquorice with? (5-4)
16. Miss Martell surrounded by funny glade on the southern tip of the Kintyre Peninsula? (9)
18. Bet earl can't respond like a ewe to a lamb! (7)
19. Shoe's side-seam made from gay rink? (7)
22. Colin out being Edinburgh scientist whose 'prism' is used for polarising light? (5)
24. Embrace using tip of tongue – then boxes! (5)

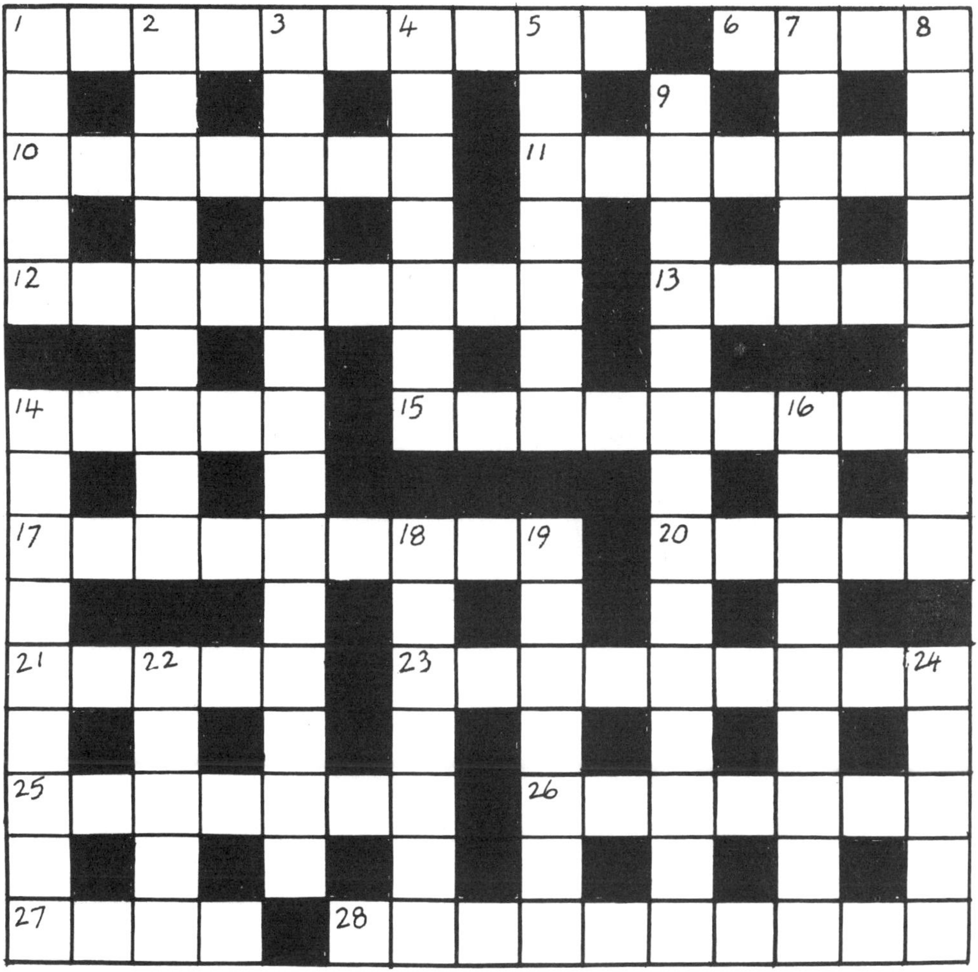

19

ACROSS

1. Bob, the sheepdog's mate, used as a bag for stealing meal from a mill spout? (5,5)
9. Scots folk-singer Robin found in part of every house? (4)
10. A tot of disorganized gin – just the thing for exposure to severe weather! (10)
11. Me and my head inside bad bag – crucial point in a game of snooker? (4-2)
12. Ban role to be played at Midlothian village? (7)
15. Rest 'ere! It's going to become rougher! (7)
16. Flighty, talkative women disturb the guts of Scotlands capital! (5)
17. Gap appearing in pending acknowledgement? (4)
18. Marie Lawrie – in a word! (4)
19. Can the recovery of damages in a Scottish court happen again? (5)
21. It takes a friend to affirm that it is idle talk! (7)
22. 'Royal' member of Edinburgh's speedway team? (7)
24. Give away own goal – but still remain cheerful! (6)
27. Grim land about Ur? Hardly when it is one of the most beautiful gardened houses in Dumfriesshire! (10)
28. Tay returns north, having been struck sharply on the knuckles! (4)
29. Title of the first part of the Trilogy by Lewis Grassic Gibbon known as "The Scots Quair" (6, 4)

DOWN

2. Scottish journalist and novelist, born in Selkirk in 1844, among whose works are "Myth, Ritual & Religion" and "The Making of Religion" (4)
3. Drink to a revengeful beating? (6)
4. I beg Len to sort out someone in rage! (7)
5. Scots taken, by the sound of it, with Royal Highland Burgh? (4)
6. Could little pigs be the same as large casks? (7)
7. Critic of one drink mixed? Run to the hills between East Lothian and Berwickshire! (10)
8. Course architect widening fairway could also be a shout to Scots goalkeeper! (5,5)
12. P.S. is Govan B, anywhere near soft-swellings affecting horses legs? (3–7)
13. Fall behind on backward nag being watery area of Easter Ross? (4,6)
14. One who frequents parties could never be an insider! (5)
15. Play the guitar to the sound of the bagpipes, perhaps? (5)
19. Cures can sometimes seem red about! (7)
20. Cor! like a beach full of pebbles! (7)
23. Pays up ad-man's fines? (6)
25. Surname of the Scots author who died in 1974 and whose first published work was 'The Grey Coast' in 1926. (4)
26. Bobbin for thread has a small whisky round reel-head! (4)

1 2 3 4 5 6 7 8
9
10
11
12 13 14 15
16
17 18
19 20
21 22 23
24 25 26
27
28
29

20

ACROSS

1. Little cottage up inside, bad risk of becoming strained refuse from fat? (8)
5. Disorderly mob sounding like a musical instrument! (6)
9. Scottish county which won the Epsom Derby in 1888! (8)
10. Fish part – skill in finding bay in Loch Long? (6)
11. Wash and stagger after? – what a lark! (8)
12. Blinked, lost penny and became undone? – very clever! (6)
14. National sports centre situated near Largs (10)
18. Particularly strong ale has only a little value, perhaps? (10)
22. See 13.
23. Can African with herring change into a pike? (8)
24. Glasgow's capital bedecked with roses in honour of military men? (6)
25. Tor borne on the shoulders of contemporary Scots poet connected with Shetlands? (8)
26. Stuart head risen about to wither? (6)
27. Dee-cress replanted amongst the people who broke from the orthodox Church of Scotland in the 18th Century? (8)

DOWN

1. Naturally, prepared learner inside! (6)
2. Have little right about 24 sheaves of grain? (6)
3. "O, wad some pow'r the giftie gie us to see oursels as —— see us!" (Robert Burns: To a Louse) (6)
4. Ron and Len kick-about Dumfriesshire village? (10)
6. Legislation introduced by Westminster in 1704 as an ultimatum to the Scots to recognise the Hanoverian Kings or be treated as foreigners (5, 3)
7. Musically bonnie, body is then arranged to reveal organiser of first Shetland Music Festival in 1944! (4, 4)
8. A German around there can make straw rope used for holding thatch together! (8)

13, 22. Name of the popular T.V. gardening programme broadcast from Aberdeen (8, 6) . . .

15. . . . T.V. make publisher who became champion of the crofters — in the style of Ireland's Parnell – in the 1880's! (8)
16. Greg inside ages, and increases! (8)
17. Can English dragon-slayer really spring up in old Pictish fort in Easter Ross? (2, 6)
19. Nazi diarist adds point to house-wall, through which enquiries may be made! (6)
20. Like it? Popular highlander might! (6)
21. Crushes tin – nags, going mad! (6)

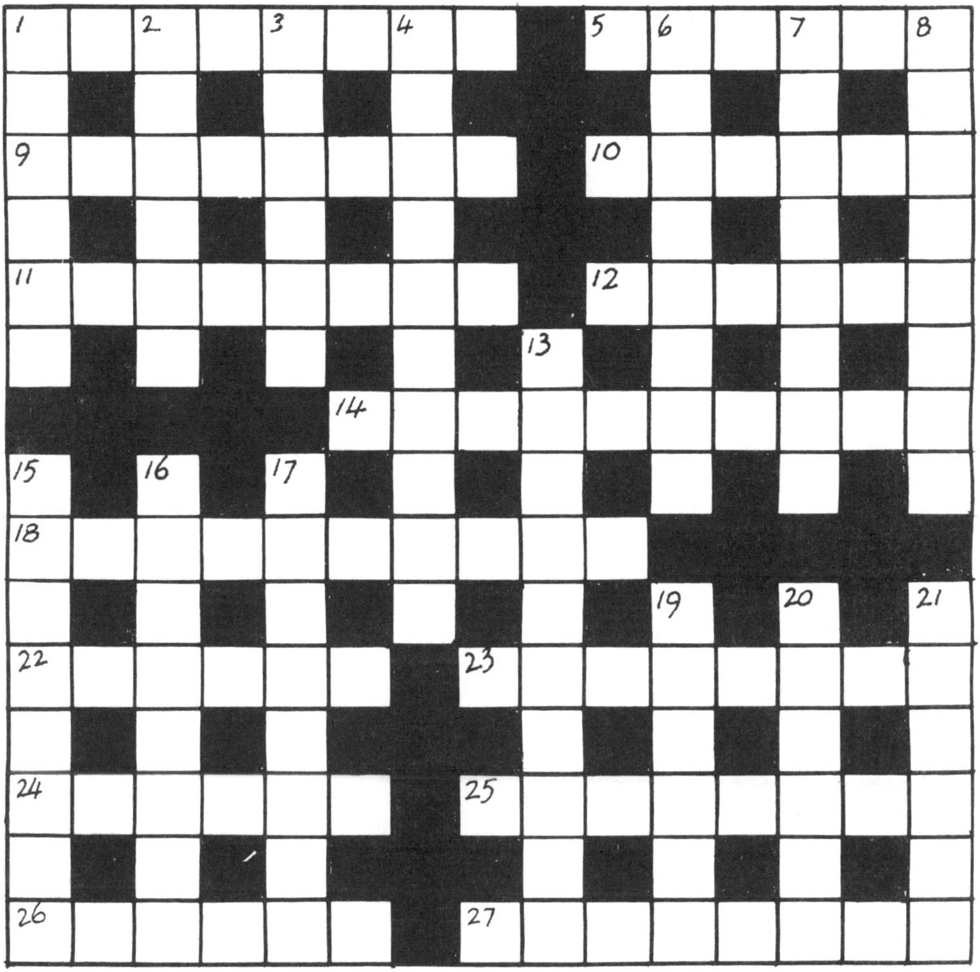
1
2
3
4
5
6
7
8
9
10
11
12
13
14
15
16
17
18
19
20
21
22
23
24
25
26
27

21

ACROSS

3. Green sloth seen around Fifeshire new town? (10)
8. Err — cake crumbling in the hands of the farmer getting so much per acre? (6)
9. Mite goes through change but still remains a small creature! (4)
10. Scotland's greatest book-binder who lived and worked in Edinburgh in the 18th Century (5,5)
11. Ground grain found in a little part of Old Meldrum? (3)
13. Can a stinger ever be alone? (4)
14. See 24.
15. Old king who has money? (4)

17,3 down, 30. Nom-de-plume of James Leslie Mitchell, author of "A Scots Quair" (5,7,6)

20. Leg in plaster? Flog it! (5)
22. Highlands dance in reverse? — rather! (4)

24,14. Popular name given to the Scottish football side of 1928 who beat England 5-1 (7,7)

25. Credit, errors excepted, flowing through S.W.Scotland beautifully! (4)
27. Nae return for a yearling? (3)
28. B.R.sail seen in Stirlingshire village? Reputed scene of battle between Scots and Romans? (10)
29. Returning see English and use to good effect! (4)
30. See 17.
31. Christian festival former Secretary of State for Scotland celebrates just north of the Caledonian Canal? (6,4)

DOWN

1. Board game with a stunted tree? (8)
2. Mourn the death of the other 'McDiarmid'? (6)
3. See 17 across.
4. Lone learner can become 'capital of Buchan' in Aberdeenshire? (5)
5. I rat about professor who, in 1911, held the first chair of rhetoric and English literature at Glasgow University! (4)
6. It's Rank, Hovis MacDougall, I mean to give a thrashing to! (8)
7. Sounds like animal land joined to Oban by 'Atlantic Bridge'? (4,4)
12. Could little Elizabeth change into a piece of soot? (4)
14. "The flowers of the forest are a' — awa' " (Anon: The flowers of the forest) (4)
16. Greasy could be another word for flattering, perhaps? (4)
17. Were clan responsible for taking all 10 English wickets in Scotland-England cricket match played in 1849? (8)
18. I was mens champion in corpulence! (8)
19. Fishing area found under a curling stone? (4)
21. The French number Govan-based part of Banffshire? (8)
23. Cricket score oil producers make into fields owned alternatively by different farmers! (3-4)
25. Essential bit of fishing is past being put aside as useless! (4-2)
26. Midlothian village, birthplace of 18th century poet, Joseph Mitchell (5)
28. Ferocious animal fed on four-rowed barley? (4)

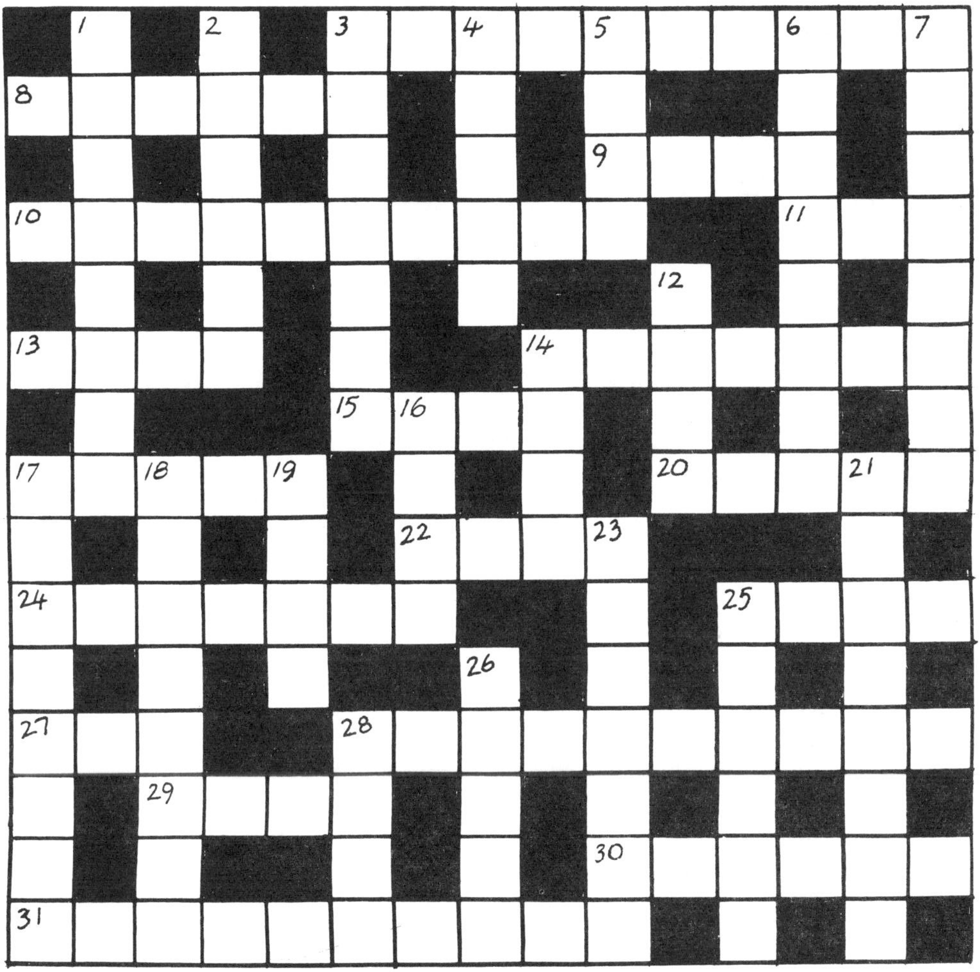
1
2
3
4
5
6
7
8
9
10
11
12
13
14
15
16
17
18
19
20
21
22
23
24
25
26
27
28
29
30
31

22

ACROSS

1. Re. Margo being a ransacker! (7)
5. Cat paw you sound like mixing for a mid-day refreshment? (4-3)
9. See 29.

10, 13 down, 12. Title of the lament composed by Pipe-major Riddle of the Scots-Guards as a tribute to his fallen comrades of the Falkland Islands conflict (3, 5, 1, 10, 8)

11. Having a great tactician, attack the Scots? (6)
12. See 10.
14. Hockey position running water into a house through its foundations, perhaps? (5)
15. Get Trudie set up with the power of speech? (9)
18. Best perm a point about when to run the Ayr Gold Cup, for example? (9)
20. I lose the Scots inventor of logarithms and get a head! (5)
22. Lew maker? otherwise tool or instrument! (4–4)
24. Can male voices really be found as the cross-bars between chair legs? (6)
26. French cheese hard? use it for cleaning doorstep! (4–5)
27. That part of the British Empire governed by the Marquis of Dalhousie between 1784 and 1801 (5)
28. Nae nuts? holy companion of Columba with a prized hand-bell at Insh! (2, 5)

29, 9. Seek ink liner around flood plain near Antonine Wall at Inveravon? (7, 5)

DOWN

1. Affairs of maist kirk? (3–2–4)
2. Old Scots Queen not returning to Angus parish? (7)
3. Clean 'gers coming from Perthshire village? (9)
4. A quarter of a year there returning without point! (4)
5. "——— Saturday Night" famous title by Robert Burns (3, 7)
6. Morar, Rannoch, and an island in the Firth of Clyde? (5)
7. Working with the left, wheel part gets help! (3–4)
8. In coming away, form opinion that is pulling! (5)
13. See 10.
16. Between 1716 & 1774 Edinburgh science club from Kean-Nairn mix up? (9)
17. House near Leuchars, Fife built round peers vestibule, perhaps? (9)
19. Free-pit, having reached the age of 21? (7) . . .
21. . . . age drop – push it with a stick! (7)
22. The Common Ragwort – Spider's place is ideal for it! (5)
23. Mostly losing a pane of glass? (5)
25. Arrange resistance with key to ferment? (4)

1
2
3
4
5
6
7
8
9
10
11
12
13
14
15
16
17
18
19
20
21
22
23
24
25
26
27
28
29

23

ACROSS

1. Does 'X' mark the rocky spot commemorating an early battle near the village of Spittalfield, Perthshire? (10)
6. Forward, and saucy, area of Angus? (4)
10. Second fee given for a puny child? (7)
11. Man often seen in paddy-field, perhaps? (7)
12. Making a sermon bigger? (9)
13. See 3.
14. Former Daily Record hero has an enclosure for catching salmon! (5)
15. Lent mates over a hire-purchase payment? (9)
17. Beard grows right in the middle of straightening out gin, sprouting! (9)
20. Can Scot heraldically conceal successive word? (5)
21. Actress Hird in Midlothian village mix-up? (5)
23. Reputedly the most beautiful of the Angus valleys – unwanted on the lawn we hear! (4, 5)
25. Blest an unusual Holy man who came to Perthshire from Bute to found many Christian settlements there around A.D. 600! (2, 5)
26. Learner or loon? That adds up to someone lost in love! (3–4)
27. The one arrangement which is easy! (4)
28. Winch a wasp away for an arms exhibition? (10)

DOWN

1. A straw-basket can be comfortable, we hear (5)
2. Loch Tiree has to be removed to Ayrshire village! (9)

3, 13. Title and name of the knighted Edinburgh-born author, among whose works are "Brigadier Gerard" and "A Study in Scarlet" (3, 6, 5, 5)

4. Easter Ross initially gets invovled in a live part of year sometimes containing Easter! (7)
5. I girn at being encircled! (7)
7. Compass point which sailor Blyth must follow with an exclamation of longing? (5)
8. Can a torturer also carry an instrument for making toast? (9)
9. Don't kill a crazy, angry religious symbol found on Islay and dating from around 800 A.D.! (9, 5)
14. Bore is age enough to get a kiss! (9)
16. Conch hero has to shell out being neither one thing nor another! (3, 3, 3)
18. I wangle around the fireside? (5–2)
19. Must Neil lug around valley of the Cairngorms? (4, 3)
22. Important Hebridean port loses right to bodily sensation? (5)
24. We nag over the appointment of this man by James II as hereditary sheriff of Wigton? (5)

24

ACROSS

1, 9. Stirring Scots song probably written to commemorate the Duke of Argyll's part in the battle of Langside in 16th century (9, 3, 6)
6. So 'ger gets organized and becomes Heather's partner? (5)
9. See 1.
10. Scotland's capital gets help from famous Scottish band leader? (5)
12. Direction food goes in makes one fat and contented? (5)
13. Happy Catholic service celebrated every August in Irvine, Ayrshire? (5-4)
14. Aspen chopped up on picturesque Inverness-shire river? (5)
16. That is, matters come to a head over a quantity of small objects? (9)
19. Bare chair seen around top of Inverness-shire peak? (9)
20. For example, nip returns to whine! (5)
21. Looks like we need a kitchen, for example, for space enough to swing the arms? (5-4)
23. Inciter found on poultry-farm perhaps? (5)
26. Try about a little Irish becoming angry? (5)
27. Ring or Mac will destroy famous Scots mountain! (9)
28. Eric Lafferty conceals the part of a tree where the branches separate! (5)
29. Warn – divers hat is off! (9)

DOWN

2. Part of Strathclyde where you can have a double right to an island? (5)
3. Sheep can't remake a prehistoric monument! (4-5)
4. Intimate friends can be the same – and yet not the same! (4)
5. Name of Scotland's youngest-ever Olympic medallist – achieved in Moscow 1980 (6, 9)
7. Upset hog sends morning letters to a celt! (5)
8. Shetland district found on the beach and in the bee? (9)
11. The refuse of fish-livers after oil extraction sounds fantastic – dosen't it? (5)
15. The name given to 'boards' set up in Scotland in 1845 to look after the 'Parish Poor' (9)
17. Ancient lairdship of the Innes family near Grange, Banffshire – starts capitally but finishes up mostly tight! (9)
18. "——wirry" a serenade given to old people marrying again (5)
22. Sounds like a sod of a river in Inverness-shire? (5)
24. The point of weapons? Complains bitterly! (5)
25. I rue about Viscount Stonehaven's large estate in Kincardineshire? (4)

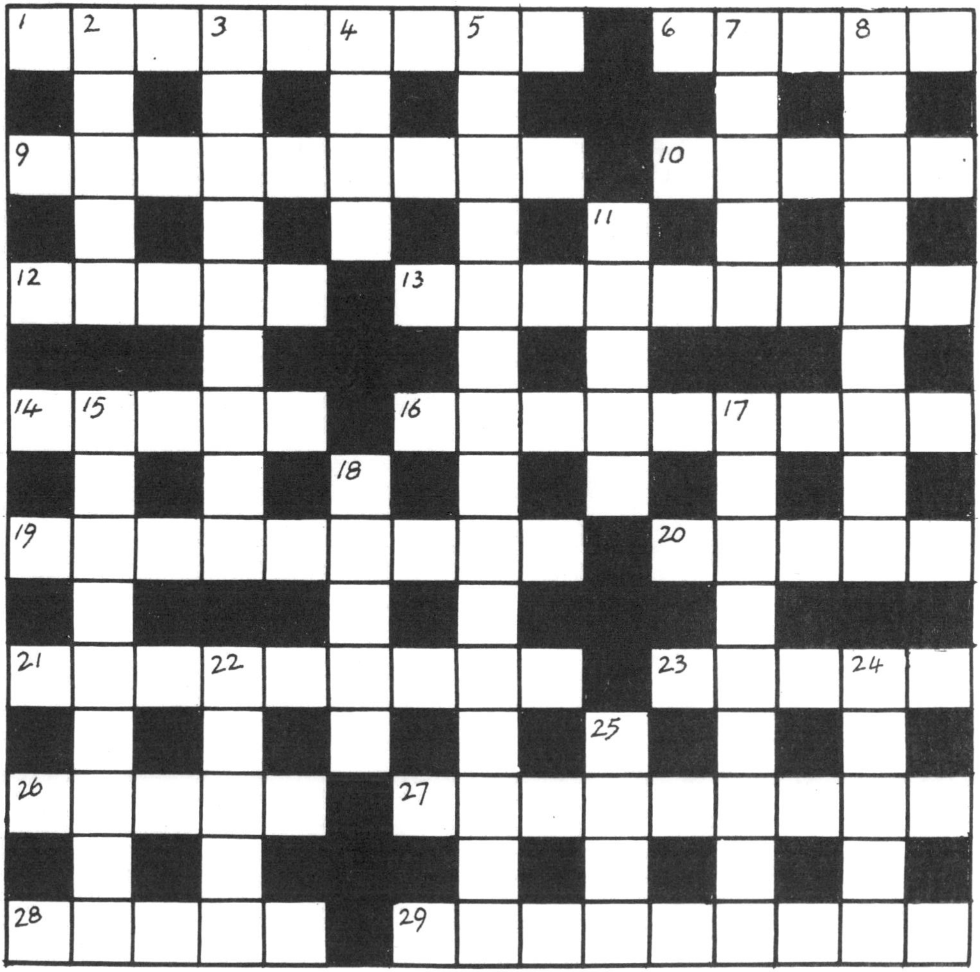
1
2
3
4
5
6
7
8
9
10
11
12
13
14
15
16
17
18
19
20
21
22
23
24
25
26
27
28
29

25

ACROSS

1. Burnt at hot parish near Inverbervie in Kincardineshire? (10)
6. Beat the drum like little Robert, we hear! (4)
10. B. Rail upset at having no station in Ayrshire village? (5)
11. Name of the former chairman of Scottish Express Newspapers who was awarded the C.B.E. in the 1983 New Years Honours List (3, 6)
12. Sharks e.g., make bird noises! (8)
13. Hastened to South Africa – just like Arran river? (5)
15. City which musically we all belong to? (7)
17. Let Barr be knocked down and rebuilt in Stirlingshire? (7)

19, 24. A1 channel a mile off the island lying near the S.W. coast of Mull! (6, 1, 8)

21. How a bun can help a fiddler! (3-4)
22. First fight flab all round then blow! (5)
24. See 19.
27. Scottish football ground good too, for hill watchers? (9)
28. Famous Edinburgh hall requires guide? (5)
29. One can be a basic ingredient of a Burns supper! (4)
30. F.C. sells key player – because he's playing weakly! (10)

DOWN

1. Name of the Pictish king who, in the 10th century, took control of the Strathclyde and Lothian regions (4)
2. Dark room required to develop district of Edinburgh? (9)
3. Point last rite given again to island weather station? (5)
4. Recognised by Scots as the "father of the fiddle". He lived between 1727 and 1807 (4, 3)
5. Set line again before showing loss? (7) . . .
7. . . . A gift can be overhead! (5)
8. Surname of the Scots author, born in Edinburgh 1825, died Rome 1894 whose works include "Martin Rattler" and "The Coral Island" (10)
9. Frightens birds away with two cars going off in the direction of Stranraer? (8)
14. Mother of Robert Burns who died in 1820 aged 88 (5, 5)
16. Animal stumbled over Arran's highest point! (4, 4)
18. Shaves in funny solution and disappears! (9)
20. Attribute change to cave, sir! (7)
21. The bittern takes a sinister stroll, we hear! (7)
23. Loch near Inverness looking like the remnants of coal-fire, we hear! (5)
25. Surname of 'Sir Robert' who, in 1527, "Exercisit The Gowf" and thereby became one of its founders (5)
26. Station point between Glasgow and Edinburgh! (4)

1
2
3
4
5
6
7
8
9
10
11
12
13
14
15
16
17
18
19
20
21
22
23
24
25
26
27
28
29
30
A
S
H
I
E

26

ACROSS

1. They usually need recreation to play football on! (5,8)
8. Bach met crazy Thane of Cawdor? (7)
9. Dried in redeveloped suburb of Edinburgh? (7)
11. Declare positively on river in Easter Ross? (6)
13. Greece and southern region initially combine to provide scourger? (8)
15. Bagpipes into a false sense of security, perhaps? (5)
16. Was Tell a Scotsman from near Stranraer? (7)
18. Lab returns to evil doings on the MacKenzie estate near Conon in Easter Ross! (7)
19. Sounds as though either a push or wheel would make this part of the Outer Hebrides go places! (5)
21. Had calls arranged over flat pieces of fertile land? (8)
23. Stairhead has ready arrangement for the Orkney farming area where norse King Sigurd is buried! (6)
25. Crazy Tex has about the last word on being tested? (7)

26, 17. Historic border church founded by King David I in the 12th century (7, 5)

28. Fetched yard to vessel sitting at east-coast port? (8, 5)

DOWN

2. Watery part of Argyllshire is reached by highland pass – back, then German salute! (4–3)
3. Fifeshire loch full of minerals? (3)
4. Cause pain in the MacHendrie Clan? (4)
5. Last (by the sound of it) Englishman's home stands as a ruin of unknown origin in Monikie, Angus! (4,6)
6. Girl rising between two points gives Labour M.P. for Midlothian! (5)
7. Gait Orr must show when having the Judge pronounce his sentence? (7)
8. i.e. Bull had me climbing over West Highland peak? (5, 6)
10. Kirkwall Castle, built in the 16th Century and fit for more than a third ranking peer? (5, 6)
12. Blackbird has louse in turmoil! (5)
14. Loch Vietch untangled a sailor's knot! (5–5)
17. See 26.
18. Bag liar must sort out to find site of old cattle fair near Balfron, Stirlingshire! (7)
20. More air needed refreshening for a sizable estate of the Innes family near Banchory, Kincardineshire? (7)
22. Feu up in most of Ayr? – It's always drunk! (3–2)
24. Mary rearranges her cupboard? (4)
27. Yell is mostly disarranged pasture-land! (3)

27

ACROSS

1. Line of attack – it's alive! (6)
4. N.B. grouse may become a coarse linen cloth! (8)
9. Grab us about the rafters of a house? (6)
10. I made rub-out and drank famous whisky liqueur? (8) . . .
12. Within Minto burn? (4)
13. Saint embraces little child? – a stupid clumsy fellow! (5)
14. Clear-sighted force – member? (4)
17. Scene of the first evening horserace meeting in 1947 (8, 4)
20. Ancient Scottish title whose ancestral home, Rires Castle was destroyed in 1402 by the Duke of Rothesay (4, 2, 6)

23, 1 down. "———— water" title of Gavin Maxwell's famous book about an otter in the West Highlands (4, 2, 6)

24. Athletic instrument doesn't get in a blow! (5)
25. A number refuse to come out of Stirlingshire burgh – but do! (4)
28. Girl gone? Sounds like she's in south west Scotland (8)
29. Mourn a farm-overseer? (6)
30. Ease nets over perforated pebbles? (8)
31. Golfer Brian sounds like what Wallace burned at Ayr! (6)

DOWN

1. See 23.
2. Member and I get little Timothy shares in the movables left to him on his fathers death? (8)
3. Dismiss Scot for spoiling milk in sultry weather? (4)
5. F.T. prefers hat strangely to spa resort in Easter Ross? (12)
6. Northern Ireland politician with a very small piece? (4)
7. Cure-all without end – arrange to become fearless! (6)
8. Scots glad, for example, returning to glance at! (6)
11. Scottish duke with king's house? It's a famous Pitlochry Hotel! (6, 6)
15. Sound like stone and is sound! (5)
16. Wooden – indefinite number attached to source of wood! (5)
18. Northumbrian river flowing through, seen outside for seventeen years? (8)
19. A spy sets a trap for dirty, slatternly women? (8)
21. Wet with T-lager spilt? (6)
22. Fifty-one sing about the English spoken in northern England? (6)
26. Scots isle a nationalist can be proud of? (4)
27. Roar about a single woman? (4)

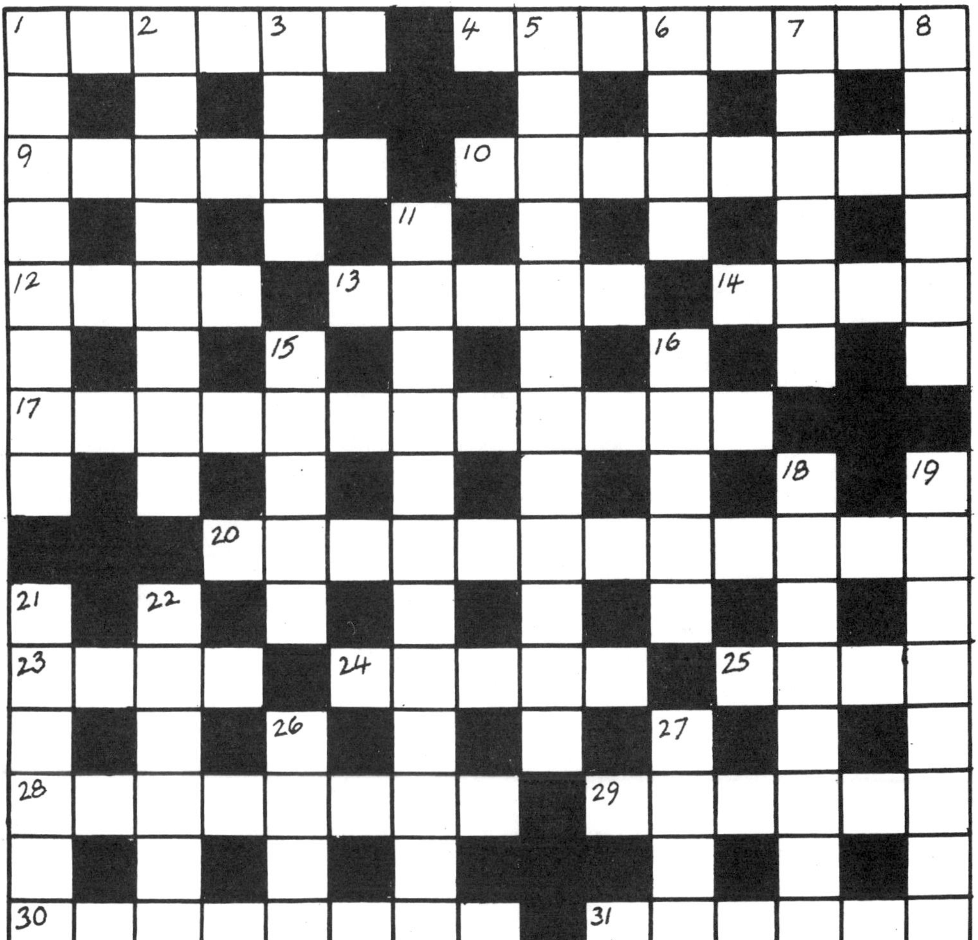

28

ACROSS

1. Pick hun out – he's a short, stout strong person! (7)
5. A Glasgow Rangers general manager with a peculiar gait by the sound of it! (7)
9. Mountain-ash doubling as a flake of wool? (5)
10. A farm doing the hard work? (9)
11. R and stews? Home of R and A! (2, 7)
12. Bessie Braddock conceals Aberdeenshire village? (5)
13. Yeast rising giving successful Edinburgh born playwright and novelist? (5)
15. A train for King Duncan, perhaps? (5, 4)
18. Actor Donald is a delight? (9)
19. Unask? undone over a disease affecting the throat of fowls fed on hot food! (5)
21. Old film actor Jackie plays the part of the common guillemont! (5)
23. I am pup – see me turn into a pet sheep! (6–3)
25. Remote part of Kintyre requires to be reached by motor and a valley by the sound of it! (9)
26. Hit about one hundred and fifty being dizzy? (5)
27. They are bending a flexible twig! (7)
28. Spin eye around being prim and proper? (7)

DOWN

1. Former Banffshire fishing burgh – just the place to drink a little chinese sauce? (7)
2. Ben Watt the French arrange in an historic Lothians abbey! (9)
3. Spared then laugh at little Edmund? (5)
4. Ayrshire estate of the Fergusson family has Kerr in a rebuilt kiln! (9)
5. Spider's home is the Scots common ragwort? (5)
6. Mull raned over the Maybole farming area! (9)
7. Former boyfriends, we hear indulging in hysterics? (5)
8. Early Glasgow has great mix-up caused by being over burdened! (7)
14. Has tin case opened up for Englishman? (9)
16. Eel-prey N.E. about to become pin used in children's Christmas game called 'tee-totum' (4–5)
17. A morsel laughs at becoming crooks? (9)
18. Hoy crop – crazy name to call a cow! (7) and . . .
20. The lies about a Shetland pony? (7)
22. All-right – it's up to Noah's boat arranged, lit a red dye? (5)
23. Landing found in the middle of picturesque Ayrshire village? (5)
24. I kill a part of the Inner Hebrides? (5)

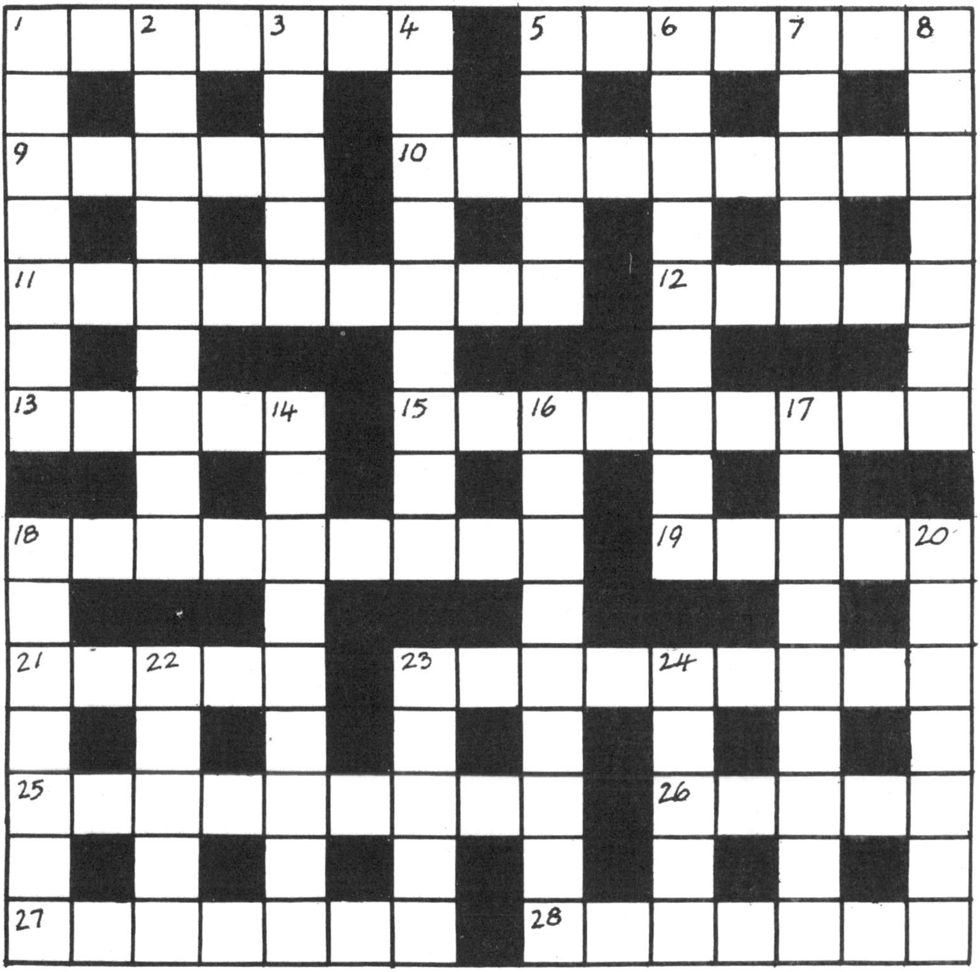
1 2 3 4 5 6 7 8
9 10
11 12
13 14 15 16 17
18 19 20
21 22 23 24
25 26
27 28

29

ACROSS

3. Ayrshire town which had a famous master, according to R.L. Stevenson (10)
8, 9. Where you may see the Lion Rampant near Doune, Stirlingshire? (6, 4)
10. See 26.
11. Slippery fish ceasing to give milk? (3)
13. "See the front o' battle ——," (Robert Burns: Scots Wha Hae) (4)
14. Rustic terra-firma skill? (7)
15. The line of grass cut by a mower – it is small, quickly said? (4)
17. I find myself in the middle of first garden, being industrious (5)
20. Builder – member of "clandestine" society originating near Kilwinning? (5)
22. Talk at length about a quantity of paper? (4)
24. Almost betray church in the Borders? (7)
25. The consequence of betting figures? (4)
27. Andrew Ritchie – head of Scots country-woman's organization? (1, 1, 1)
28. A little altitude on inside of chill part of Edinburgh? (6, 4)
29. Clackmannanshire burgh where wartime broadcaster Lidell came from, we hear? (4)
30. See 26.
31. Short of hats? – name given in the carse of Gowrie to cup-shaped fungi (6–3)

DOWN

1. See 14.
2. Draw C.O. on historic Nairnshire village? (6)
3. Sir Ben's out of Aberdeenshire estate bought by General Gordon in 1815? (7)
4. Tadpole found in soup spoon? (5)
5. Paws ground for the curlews! (4)
6. Aros, Kyle get confused about their short cloaks? (8)
7. Met noble excitedly on border bay? (8)
12. A man's return? – greedily snap at! (4)
14, 1. Rothesay-born child star of musical presentations (4, 8)
16. Fuss about Ipswich and Scotland World Cup forward? (4)
17. Could bamboo be found in the district around Eaglesham? (8)
18. Raid a lad was confused about in old Argyll? (8)
19. With ex-Hibernian manager he's a devil! (4)
21. Cold about moon? – name for the beautiful house of Fraser-Tytler family near Dores in Inverness-shire! (3, 5)
23. "R.S. ——" Scottish based newsagents (7)
25. Sham, go about old Celtic letters (6)
26, 10, 30. Famous Scottish song composed after the defeat of the Jacobite forces under "Bonnie Prince Charlie' (5, 10, 6)
28. A hundred fix hat then strike ball with fist! (4)

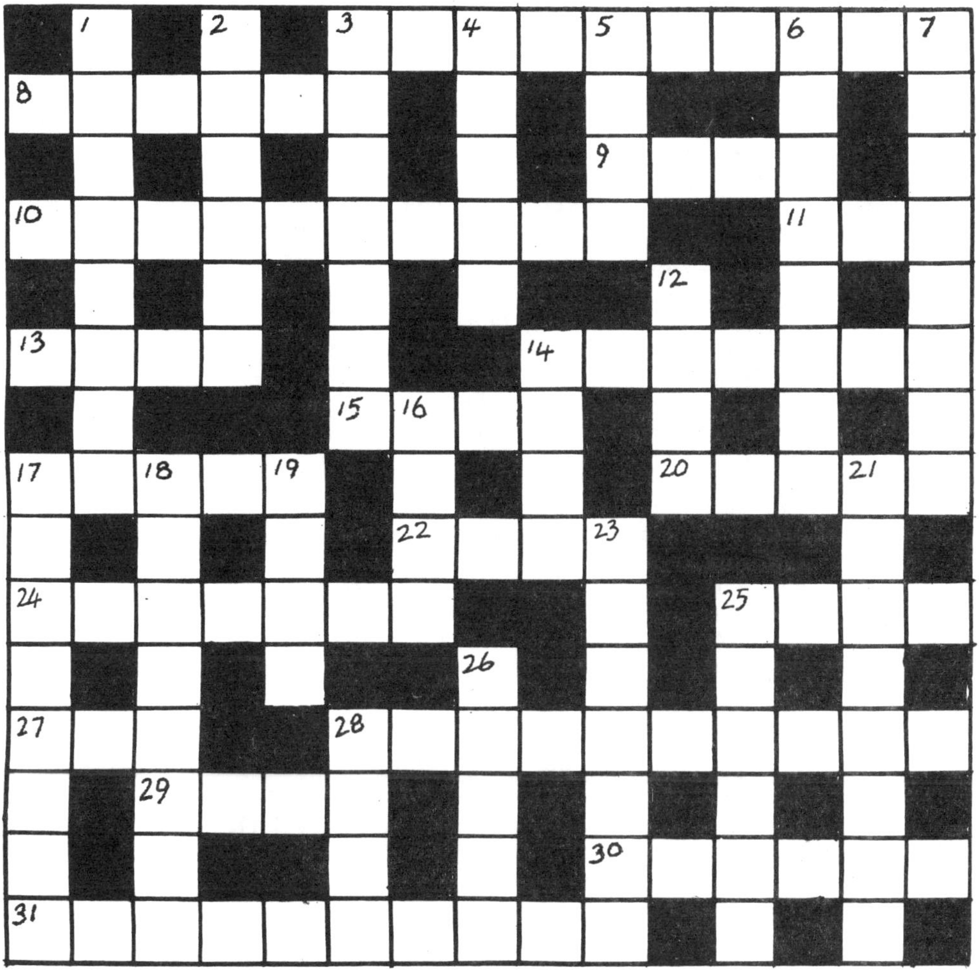
1
2
3
4
5
6
7
8
9
10
11
12
13
14
15
16
17
18
19
20
21
22
23
24
25
26
27
28
29
30
31

30

ACROSS

1. By right Scots Loch should be attached to Northumbrian border hamlet! (7)
5. Free but mostly dull arrangement, how sad? (7)
9. The complete abstainer? (5)
10. Male ruin'd? it's a fake castle near Culross in Fifeshire! (9)
11. Except the state of having just removed some clothing? (6)
12. Feline's group having some eye trouble? (8)
14. Ann confused – not available as grand-mother? (5)
15. Canine idiot that is a sea-bird? (3–6)
18. Title of a Burns poem whose first line is "There was on a time, but old time was then young," (9)
20. Angus village that is after the confusion? (5)
22. With Latin breed about hands can be numbed? (8)
24. I do wrong – Glasgow's boundaries making the silverings of a looking-glass? (6)
26. Renfrewshire burgh where senior churchmen do not tell the truth about it being Sir William Wallace's birthplace? (9)
27. A golf term prior to a bad shot? (5)
28. "Mull of——" Wings flew high here! (7)
29. Overburdened – carry little Gertrude on back? (7)

DOWN

1. B.C. coin the confused daughter of King Malcolm II and mother of King Duncan made? (6, 3)
2. Bruce plotted on this isle more than I.R.L.? (7)
3. Burns farm home from 1789 – made up of Lille sand? (9)
4. Famous Marquis – a thick sod for burning! (4)
5. He came, according to Burns, here to woo! (6, 4)
6. Old Scots actor Alistair has me rising too – it's insecure! (5)
7. Former U.S. President adds measure to famous castle near Inverkeithing? (7)
8. Make a loan round the east – then ceased! (5)
13. Early part of Scots capital has stomach we hear for the great estate near Balfron, Stirlingshire, which was owned by John Napier, the inventor of logarithms! (10)
16. Above C.I. Gas arrangement at the far end of Loch Shin? (9)
17. Let Sheene organize the wrapping for a corpse? (4–5)
19. Surname of the one-time owner of Mount Quhanie Castle near Rathillet, Fife who heroically led the anti-Cromwellian forces in defence of Dundee in 1651 (7)
21. Famous Cheviot gorge, popular with climbers and chickens perhaps! (7)
22. Inspect the wheat ear? (5)
23. A good description of Ayrshire potatoes perhaps? (5)
25. Do you have to shout to be heard on this Shetland isle? (4)

31

ACROSS

1, 5. Major Scottish tourist attraction built in the 15th century by Thomas Cochrane, a favourite of James III (8, 6)
9. Ink verse written about part of Musselburgh where once stood a Roman camp? (8)
10. See 34.
12. A reward for being good at curling perhaps? (4–5)
14. Order Clackmannanshire county town to change end to duck! (5)
15. Lord Bannerman included a half-year stipend legally due to a deceased ministers heirs, over and above his normal dues? (3)
16. Drinking bout? – Er, involving disc (6)
19. Deter from flushing loo? (5)
22. To have legal right of recovering damages can happen again! (5)
23. Ray loses heart after rang about knotty problem? (6)
25. Rub back a fir-cone? (3)
28. In Scots law, does it have to be a teacher to look after boy under fourteen? (5)
29. Mail ruler sorts himself out on Edinburgh's highest point? (9)
32. East-South? land in the middle to see them at Blairdrummond Safari Park! (6)
33. Roman emperor who established his H.Q. at Lochore, Fifeshire in A.D. 79 (8)
34, 10. Australian city sounds heavenly? it's Scotlands leading country singer! (6, 6)
35. Editor requires ten men sorted out – it's essential! (8)

DOWN

1. His strange right to join the Royal Academy gives a picturesque glen near Laggan Bridge, Inverness-shire! (6)
2. Scottish rugby full-back coming from Ayrshire? (6)
3. Bustle and maul about Robert initially? (5)
4. Nuzzled – and sucked at the same time! (5)
6, 20. The name of three Scottish kings and several trade unionists combine to make successful Scottish theatrical attraction! (9, 8)
7. Yet learner and liar may make a good tailor? (8)
8. Look closely at the lips of east coast fishing port perhaps? (8)
11. Dad and his pal make up small island lighthouse seen off Ayr? (6)
13. Scots kidney doubling as another organ? (3)
17. Crib gored to pulp on Northumberland village station near Hadrian's wall? (9) . . .
18. Ring about the morning? We have a date in the Cheviot village in the Breamish valley! (6)
20. See 6.
21. Another rugby full-back who played for his country? (8)
24. Era about the Kirkwall-born explorer of the 19th century? (3)
26. Muse of disgusting disarray? (6)
27. A hundred stare about then tear food to pieces with their mouths! (6)
30. Helensburgh born T.V. man with middle name? (5)
31. Footpath – but listen for the orange-peel! (5)

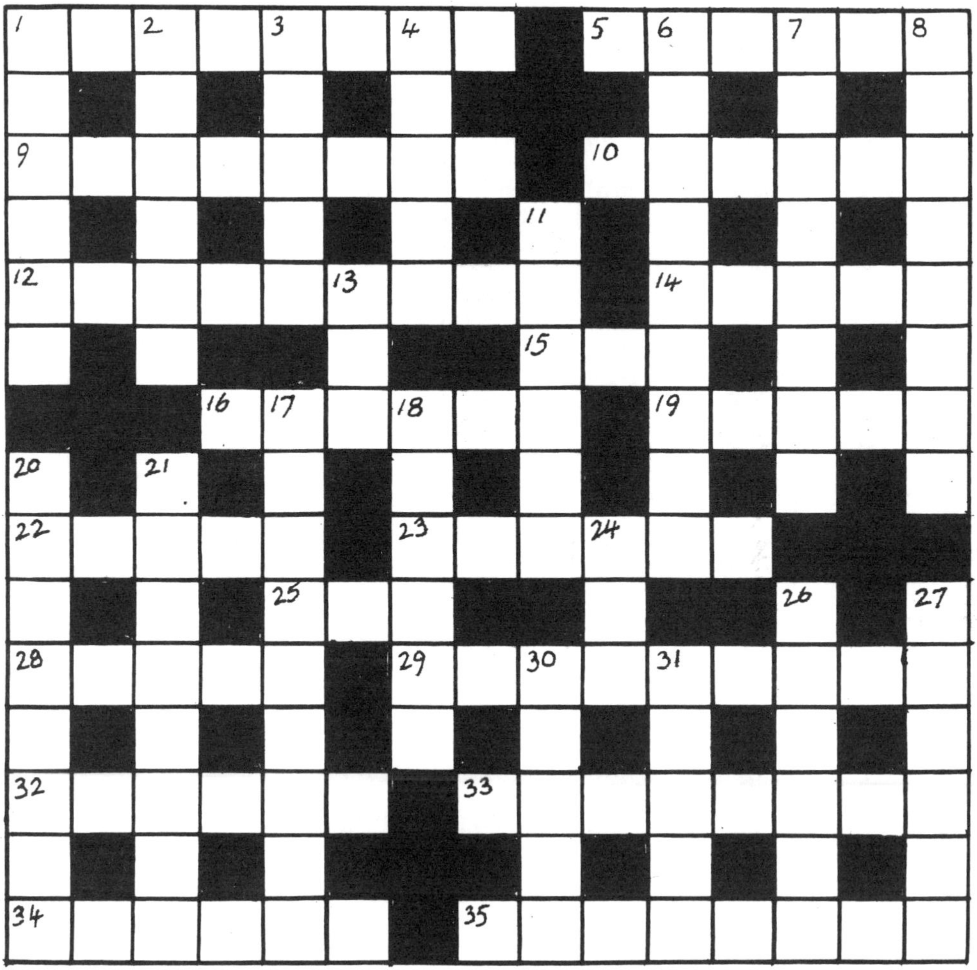

32

ACROSS

1. A lovely game of cards to be had near Cumbernauld? (11)
9. When were you first aware it included a surfeit? (4)
10. Famous Scottish air found in park in Glasgow? (11)
11. Scots undervalue an English loch? (4)
14. Learner joins rebels – disorganized making spectacles of themselves? (7)
17. Magnificent stain-glass window commemorates this official of Aberdeen in St. Machar's Cathedral church – sounds like he was indolent! (5)
18. Delicate way of putting point on kith? (5)
19. Village of Angus lying at the base of the great Buddon Point peninsula between Monifieth and Carnoustie (5)
20. Historic Scottish burgh with song separating the north from Norway? (5)
21. A torn earth-nut? (5)
22. Does it reflect the moods of certain songs? (5)
23. Only part of vinaigrette sauce need be sour! (5)
24. Mr. Flynn could come from Perthshire village in the centre of the Carse of Gowrie! (5)
25. Can Robert initially bear the expense of being in an old village in Moray? (7)
29. On the head of a judge's favourite advocate through whom interest was made for clients? (4)
32. Ace I eke lock from in order to make soup? (4-1-6)
33. "As Phoebus and the famous —— were glowrin owre my pen" (Robert Burns: Epistle to Davie, a Brother Poet) (4)
34. Parkhead side angry at seeing Scottish religious symbol (6, 5)

DOWN

2. Have an eye for the farm animal – it's a blue tit! (2-2)
3. Make a fist at a part of the church? (4)
4. Scottish politician whose name was law in 1922-23? (5)
5. That is fish eggs for a great-grandchild! (3 – 2)
6. Outer Hebridean has five at heart in setting up a gable-end! (5)
7. Fifeshire castle from then dry star? (11)
8. River utensil makes 18th century Scottish dish with salmon and herbs! (5, 6)
12. The ferocious part of the Scots ensign? (4, 7)
13. Staying in rock? – it's a Blantyre born explorer! (11)
14. Treble N.E. boisterous intermittent wind? (7)
15. Tires right in the middle of an Ayrshire burgh? (5)
16. Underwent a trial – at sea by the sound of it! (7)
19. Highland county town where you can only prohibit two fellows? (5)
26. Call away – it's all right in the middle of mill-wheel's bucket! (5)
27. Financial Times has Eisenhower in the middle – he's difficult to please! (5)
28. Ruin cleric by removing a hundred? (5)
30. Aberdeenshire abbey where venison is always on the menu? (4)
31. Cease doing something in blissful innocence? (4)

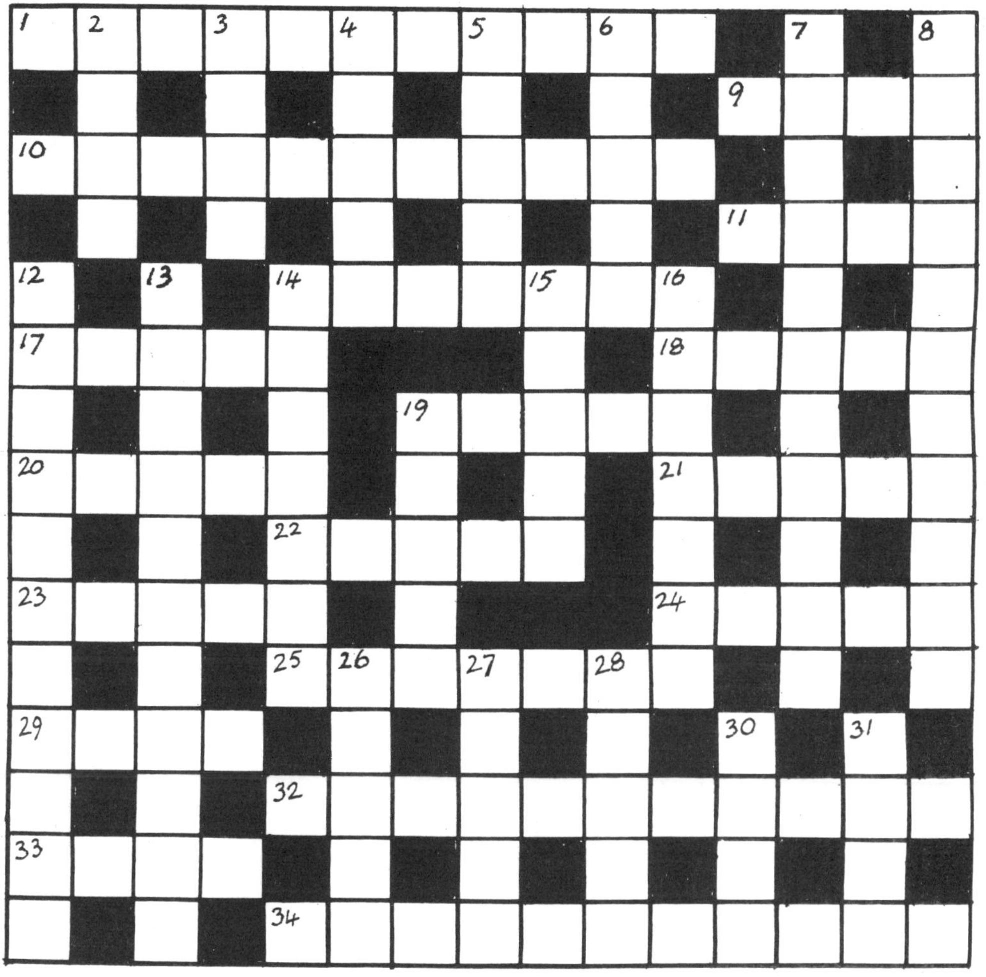

33

ACROSS

1. Lets hand tell you where the little ponies come from? (8)
5. Grinding house article may give you former Secretary of State for Scotland? (6)
9. Stretch of water of greater importance in the Highlands? (4, 4)
10. Compared first lady to little Edward? (6)
11. List pair? It's inspirational! (8)
12. By the sound of it I see Italian city surrounded by cow with crumpled horns! (6)
14. She is late – I go around Sir Walter Scott's residence near Galashiels? (10)
18. Skye Water? – blow in it! (4, 6)
22. Katrine loses head and is disorderly and ill-tempered! (6)
23. Leg is broken – in part traction to become ancient Scots earldom! (8)
24. Lament the fact that yellow-hammer loses heart? (6)
25. I rest about man – he was holy and had the first church at Crathie (near Balmoral) dedicated to him! (2, 6)
26. In rest? Upset being eager! (6)
27. Even weir must be arranged to compete with Kew as gardening paradise on the north-west coast! (8)

DOWN

1. Spend money on a patch of colour? (6)
2. Nor Ochie can amount to anything! (6)
3. About a thousand mile? Not too far for a kid! (6)
4. Worm annals trouble Fifeshire peak! (7, 3)
6. Skin ever inside about to become Roman Station near Musselburgh? (8)
7. A far-off wasteland? Just the breeding ground of a Scots golfer! (8)
8. Lovers no-one can displace from Gin dells? (8)
13. African explorer loses direction and finds New Town! (10) . . .
15. . . . not far from his birth place! (8)
16. Edinburgh-based nationalist newspaper? (8)
17. Jurymen sound like good judges of distance! (8)
19. Accuse pupils of doing it when excited! (6)
20. Object to religious instruction being included with string vest? (6)
21. Take snuff noisily! (6)

34

ACROSS

7. True lums need to be reconstructed after foreign part pays duty for those coming voluntarily to a mill? (3-4, 7)
9. Gross tonnage reconstructed with large pins? (6)
10. Decree that it is a coin with an eagle on it? (8)
11. Famous cricket commentator with rib back in area 2 miles west of Abroath? (8)
13. A cry of exasperation also given to Perthshire scene of a fierce 13th century battle between the McLarens and the Buchanans? (6)
14. Pack to the utmost having a short sharp pain? (4)
15. Mend a slap across the face? (5)
16. Mother goes quiet, having a nibble? (4)
17. Let shy lunatic say it's 'yourself'! (6)
19. Saints preserved around Luke and Lumen, the rascals! (8)
21. Earwig has famous west coast lighthouse losing lamp head in exchange for ringer? (8)
23. Obtain a statement? (6)
24. "————————, my Eppie MacNab?" first line of a Burns' short song entitled 'Eppie MacNab' (1, 3, 2, 2, 6)

DOWN

1. i.e. Scout or marsh? in perverse state! (14)
2. Scottish burgh sounds like being of good character – and is! (8)
3. Thump pigeon with a little silicon? (6)
4. Having lost point, kneed animal breathing heavily? (4)
5. Berwickshire town bus-stop in a Fifeshire village? (8)
6. Hare out on street holding drinking bout practised by the chiefs of the western isle who sat in circle until drunk! (6)
8. Work by R. L. Stevenson based on his thoughts while living in Anstruther (6, 8)
12. Set out despite being out of sorts? (5)
15. See force out after coil? it educates! (8)
16. Drink to grinding machine in Argyllshire? (8)
18. Why? Cos' it's containing fragments of broken flax! (6)
20. After hearing organ little mermaid becomes a complainer! (6)
22. Seek for a novice to dig up Tay? (4)

1
2
3
4
5
6
7
8
9
10
11
12
13
14
15
16
17
18
19
20
21
22
23
24

35

ACROSS

1. Northern Scottish county which should be near the borders by the sound of it? (10)
6. Dundee football park returns to being the shaft of a scythe! (4)
10. Race should be organized before a hundred grouse in Gaelic! (5)
11. Edinburgh suburb which is always being modernised, it seems! (9)
12. Colon's in to make sense of the sheriff who was the first man to climb Skye's tallest peak, Sgurr Alaisdair in the late 19th century! (8)
13. Reel off around 500 to make senior member of the church of Scotland? (5)
15. I say! Leg could be part of the Orkneys! (7)
17. Easter Ross village founded in 1810 has Welsh beginning and heavy end! (7)
19. The jaws sounding like passages down a mine! (7)
21. Western land where, if you look closely, you'll find Ayrshire! (7)
22. The moral part of Angus? – well, nearly by the sound of it! (5)
24. You'll find church support big in Orkney! (8)
27. Fire-maker who also keeps dogs perhaps? (9)
28. You French have the skill to make a farming area near the Trossachs! (5)
29. O'Shanter bends round uranium using the nozzle of a smithy forge! (4)
30. Vennal liar explains as that area of Moray lying to the north of Cairngorm! (10)

DOWN

1. Talk politely about a bag – and wine too! (4)
2. In returning twice teach about the village and its famous distillery in Easter Ross? (9) . . .
3. . . . and learner winds up in repeat visit to Perthshire castle? (5)
4. Scottish border clan whose motto is "Endure with Strength" (7)
5. Can Ewen compose himself and give the child his first kiss on getting his new coat? (7)
7. Used to have it written down, perhaps? (5)
8. Abbey near Castle Douglas where, in 1568, Mary Queen of Scots, spent her last night on Scottish soil (10)
9. Review an assorted beautiful whitewashed house, seat of clan Campbell, 2 miles east of Taynuilt, Argyllshire? (8)
14. Burns part-description of a mouse? (3, 7)
16. Victim of capital punishment could also be in pain! (8)
18. Believe it or not it has nine nicks in the borders! (9)
20. With tin exterior like constant touring around on bicycle (7) . . .
21. . . . A.1 rider will always wind-up in Lanarkshire burgh! (7)
23. Lend help to a northern island? (5) . . .
25. . . . a wand would not! (3–2)
26. A kind of gun used by the Scots to spring a surprise! (4)

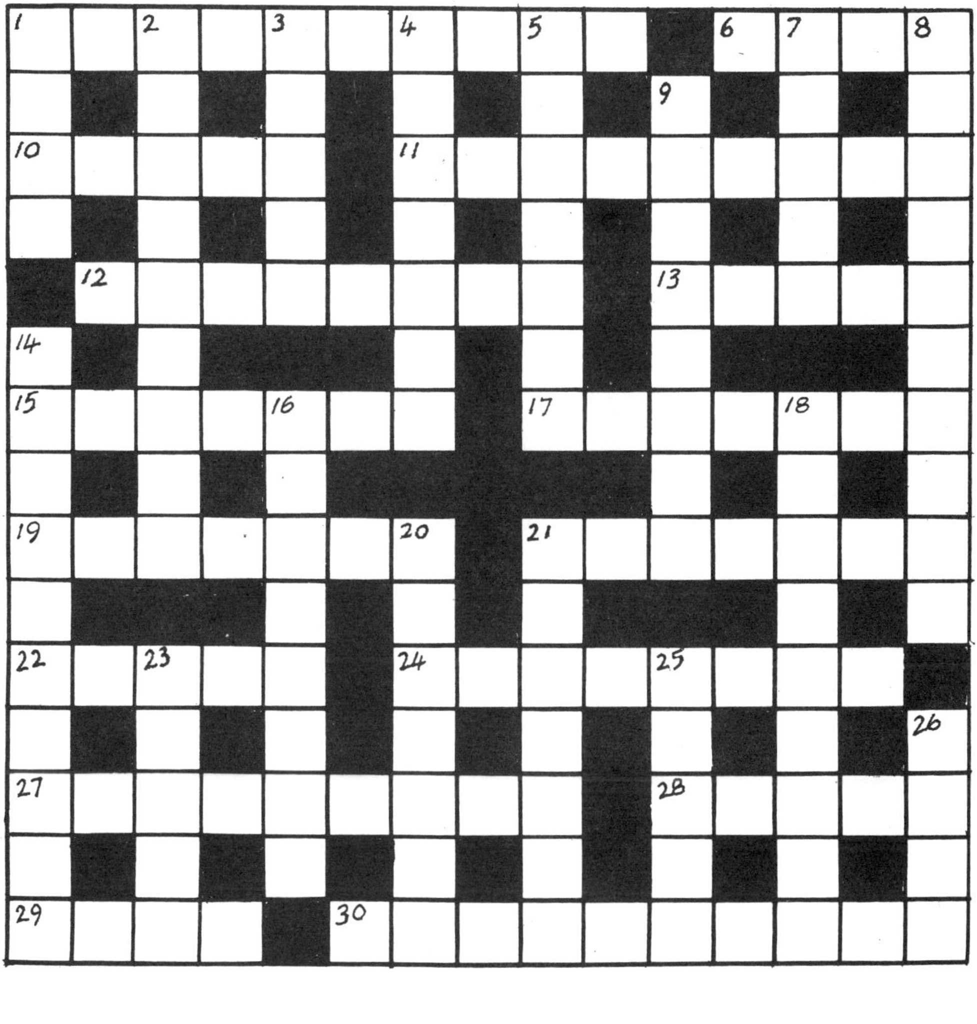
1
2
3
4
5
6
7
8
9
10
11
12
13
14
15
16
17
18
19
20
21
22
23
24
25
26
27
28
29
30

36

ACROSS

1. It could be hot, boy finds out what it's like being a Covenanter! (6, 3)
6. Its tense, diplomacy going on round Hungary! (5)
9. Lie about the French and look on it with dislike? (3–2)
10. I train in circuits before court appearance of fine wool? (6–3)
11. It's folly to hire feu! (7)
12. Link course with backward run? A dwarf might! (7)
14. Dunbartonshire town fit for a Princess and I? (10)
15. Sail along Perthshire river? (4)
18. It's easy in Caithness! (4)
19. What Prince Charles Edward Stuart is doing with the Jacobites is causing severe pain! (10)
23. A giddy young fellow is chicken, certainly! (3–4)
25. Made a hit around the mouth of the Ugie – then cleared out! (7)
26. Lanarkshire coal bing transmitting Scottish Television pictures? (9)
27. An upward break in a mineral stratum yields a mixture of energy, silver, uranium and phosphorus! (5)
28. A joint can sort out fifty-one yet! (5)
29. Part of Celtic strip advertising no-smoking zone? (5, 4)

DOWN

1. See 17.
2. Self-propelled craft? It's the mumps! (9)
3. Ado? never what you'd expect to meet driving to the highlands? (4, 4)
4. Obtuse angle Ed had made long-sighted? (4 – 3)
5. I wink at doctor – accompanying in a glass of whisky perhaps? (5, 2)
6. Set in order pig rut? (4, 2)
7. Whitehead in the middle of fuel? perhaps he's stoking-up for these highland games? (5)
8. Quite a number? well, a few! (3)
13. Deterred nag from organizing beggar's money? (4 – 7)
16. Largshire? well – that's a bone of contention! (9)

17, 1 down. A hound chancing a meal? Messy for the Gaelic Books Council! (2, 6, 11)

20. Scottish superiority at what might be called 'bowling' in cricket? (7)
21. Learner grabs hold of the middle of golf club then mixes grain, peas and oats with it! (7)
22. A strong, rough-mannered person could be dangerous, we hear! (6)
24. Loanhead lain up, waiting to be named champion in Gaelic! (5)
26. Ivy may cling to a tree just like a flying mammal! (3)

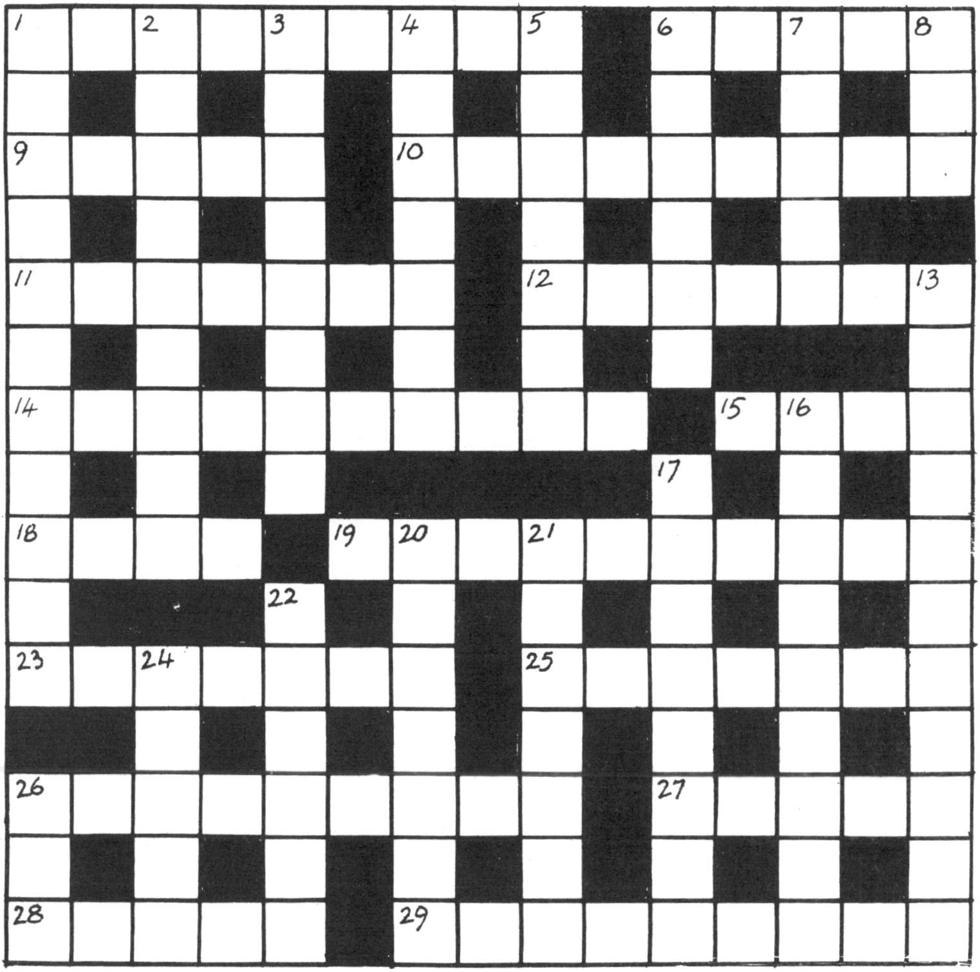

37

ACROSS

1. Give Milan back to Dunbartonshire town? (9)
8.9.14. Title and name of the former M.P. for Kinross and West Perthshire who became Prime Minister in the 1960's (3,4,7-4)
10. Important historical locality in Argyll only to be seen on horseback? (7)
13. Live rune is industrial giant with research establishment at Torry in Aberdeenshire? (8)
14. See 8.
16. Lading is e.g. an important part of the Inner Hebrides? (4,6)
20. Under-right after a single? (4)
22. A quantity of paper sounding just like a rumour? (4)
24. Magnate still going strong despite a lot of whisky! (4,6)
28. Sergeant-Major being pursued by two ducks seeks shelter in famous cave in Sutherland? (4)
29. Birds weight taken in picturesque village near Edinburgh? (8)
31. Now, — a white speck on a finger-nail as an augury of a gift? (7)
34. Row in east? Aith Lifeboat (Shetlands) named after it, serving from 1935 until 1961 (7)
35. Rugby post erected in the middle of pussy-willow completes former Glasgow football park? (7)
36. Greek is certainly not a dead language in this part of Stirling! (9)

DOWN

1. That part of Argyllshire seen going down a central tube haphazardly? (3-4)
2. Lose heart ploughing, throbbing with pain perhaps? (7)
3. Mid-Argyller? that is to say considerably! (5)
4. Victory in Europe? oil company contributed a ship! (7)
5. Inquires politely about two rivers near Montrose? (4)
6. She was formerly a tourist attraction of Loch Lomond (4)
7. Scots capital and iron and steel town combine to give jelly-fish! (7)
11. Dash about with cry of pain having fallen into a 70 ft. chasm in Finnich Glen, Stirlingshire? (6)
12. Former Foreign Secretary flowing through Fife? (4)
15. Soothe a thousand with black gold? (4)
17. The highest of the 'Arrochar Alps' seen in Crimea? (3)
18. A stone? Malta playing the game. (4)
19. Former Scottish centre-forward worshipped in the pre-reformation church at Deskford, Banffshire? (2,4)
21. Point to myself? A familiar friend! (3)
22. Helicopter practically rising straight up in a ragged coat? (7)
23. Is the Latin to be the ends of a curb-chain? (4)
25. Border castle (near Carlisle) of very little value by the looks of it! (7)
26. Eat rink wildly then swallow source of Glasgow's water supply? (7)
27. Rise man — it's what a lady is frightened of in her stocking! (3-4)
30. ... Beautiful silk got from a man in Onthank? (5)
32. Thus high school hums over a tune? (4)
33. Little Christine named after a Roman camp situated at Brechin? (4)

1 2 3 4 5 6 7
8
9
10 11 12
13
14 15
16 17 18 19 20 21
22 23 24 25 26 27
28
29 30
31 32 33
34
35
36

38

ACROSS

1. The rib of man put back as a Perthshire village? (6)
5. One of the larger Lanarkshire towns by the sound of it? (6)
8. About a fibber returning to this Fife port? (5)
9. We roll about Fifeshire looking for standing stones? (6)
10. Kite flies about article outside making "A.J." an author of the "Dictionary of the Older Scottish Tongue" published in 1980! (6)
11. Queen's insignia gets through to a grumbler? (5)
14. Halve end? Re-arrange to meet at historic mill near Carter Bar in the borders (8)
16. A site for a Scots stone incorporating snake? (6)
18. No, I dish the grand old East Lothian? (15)
20. But other half may join French king we hear to form well-knowr highland peak! (3, 3)
22. Burn near Jedburgh which may holiday on a string? (8)
25. Belch during a lively dance? (5)
27. A snack between meals? just what the doctor ordered after a change of heart! (6)
28. Perthshire river providing inspiration for The Nutcracker Suite? (6)
29. The property of Auchtermuchty? (5)
30. Can mischievous boy steal most of mum? (6)
31. Scottish rugby full back and winger can put on bridge near Hadrians Wall! (6)

DOWN

1. Piece of Scottish jewellery of historic importance in Lorn? (6)
2. A number at the end of war-retreat, afraid? (4)
3. The man to appeal to the gallery in Glasgow? (8)
4. Where whisky was only wishful thinking? (11, 4)
5. Bachelor of law makes initial sacrifice around art – and falls flat in the mud! (6)
6. Force American President has for the stalks of plants which children squirt? (4)
7. Cure in order to find Kilmarnock-born Archbishop of Canterbury? (6)
12. Did have lead stolen from outside? it's a swindle! (1, 6)
13. A new game: Soaps and Ladders! (7)
15. Dual point – Bay of Easter Ross! (5)
17. What Gipsy Rose Lee did to draw the last milk from a cow? (5)
19. Paid up then rising outside Peebles famous castle? (8)
20. Rainbow densely covering village near Melrose? (6)
21. Cheviot village around margin of England? (6) . . .
23. . . . confuses Les but then Don goes straight to nearby town? (6)
24. Could Scots author Linklater also be red? (4)
26. American car maker seen in estate village near Berwick laid out in 1859 for Lousia, Marchioness of Waterford? (4)

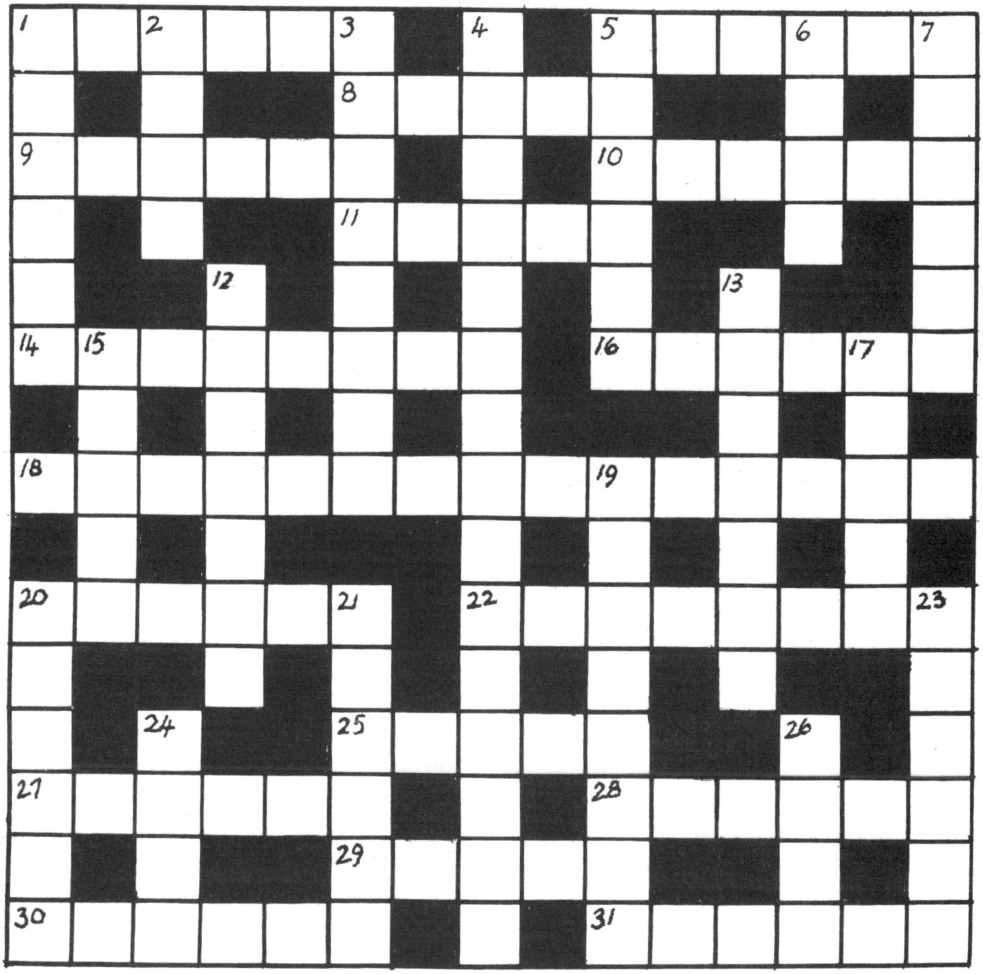

39

ACROSS

1. English city gets an opening as Lothian industrial centre? (8)
5. Living in Kansas, copper's informer cracks? (6)
9. Trip up neep, being shorter in size? (8)
10. Liz gets wet and upset seeing ruined 18th century castle standing on the River Till near Kelso! (6)
12. Surname of the Scots historiographer who wrote "Essay on the Ancient Inhabitants of Scotland" in 1729 (5)
13. English Queen who made some cutting comments on Scottish history? (9)
14. A lover of Scotland – but only since 1928? (11)
18. Laird I leg at wedding? – his coat is trailing in the mud! (7, 4)
21. Coil out? A.A. add rum and is good enough to play for Scotland and Manchester United (3, 6)
22. Ever heard of Saint Robert? he was short, backward and burst! (5)
23. Cur runs about in thy short, squat posture? (6)
24. I gleem – it is legal! (8)
25. Cares about king having landspaces? (6)
26. Eel has outstanding chance to become seen in front of fire receiving cinders? (3 – 5)

DOWN

1. Lonely Argyllshire peak around which you are to bath nine? (3, 5)
2. Hit of the north? loses right to be a towering peak in Aberdeenshire (3 – 1 – 4)
3. Shine having decided to send American soldier involved with rookie ahead of German elite? (5)
4. Title of a famous auto-biographical poem by Robert Burns (5, 3, 1, 3)
6. Start fighting again about famous Lothians abbey? (9)
7. Sleep comes after religious instruction then hesitate to add berry becoming red currant! (6)
8. St. Elcho loses nothing in becoming seal! (6)
11. Sounds like woeful old coins become children's name for small flat shells bleached by the sea! (5, 7)
15. Ancient Scotsman joins early Harlaw to become district around Aberdeen? (3, 6)
16. Galloway village with highland pub, we hear? (8)
17. He trebles – speaking double dutch? (8)
19. Initially Financial Times with a lot to do with laying pipeline to this little part of the Orkneys? (6)
20. Whir round with stone? sounds like the Brent-goose (6)
22. I am at the heart of little 13 across trying to reach Ayrshire town (5)

1
2
3
4
5
6
7
8
9
10
11
12
13
14
15
16
17
18
19
20
21
22
23
24
25
26

40

ACROSS

1. Big banana feet? (5, 8)
10. "Hope, for a season, bade the world farewell, and —— shrieked as Kosciusko fell!" (Thomas Campbell: The Pleasures of Hope) (7)
11. Article: highland farm as restored church between Doddington and Berwick? (7)
12, 13. Break clan? reconstructed R.L. Stevenson hero! (4, 5)
14. Surname of the border poet also known as "The Ettrick Shepherd" sounds more like a pig-man to me! (4)
17. Mild din? – very mediocre! (7)
18. Large border river and the French play the bagpipes? (7)
19. A recent grinding machine standing near Keith in Banffshire? (7)
22. Cromarty's other half within one Italian composer? (7)
24, 16 down. Uncaged birds who were Irish mercenaries who fought for Bonnie Prince Charlie in 1745? (4, 5)
25. Fixes stakes into the ground – with a dagger? (5)
26. The smart and active may be good at a little branch of mathematics (4)
29. Lady Rosebery hitting bell and finding means of escape from danger? (7)
30. Three ducks lent, to be cooked and held in high esteem? (6 – 1)
31. The name given to a major English-Scottish battle of 1575 commemorated in many border tapestries (9, 4)

DOWN

2. "Scotland is the name of what you call ——" (R.L. Stevenson: Catriona) (7)
3. "The —— of the Lake" 1810 novel by Sir Walter Scott (4)
4. Cream spilt on medical hero of A.J. Cronin? (7)
5. The shortest way to a close shave? (4 – 3)
6. Inverness-shire loch found in Mesazoic hardstone? (4)
7. Led around liquid pool, the king of the Belgians who often lived on Kinrara estate near Alvie in Inverness-shire from 1821 onwards!(7)
8. "—— —— —— Guilford good" Burns song usually sung to the tune 'Black Watch' (1, 8, 4)
9. Drunken shilling? only for a very young calf! (10 – 3)
15. Rib out about the French girl? Bleat like a sheep! (5)
16. See 24 across.
20. Law overturned then tie lace of famous Scots outlaw! (7)
21. In disappearing with learner Lothian burgh becomes major Scottish shipyard founder? (7)
22. Being lab, Brer has to be made into a quick reader! (7)
23. Ire Isla shows at a Jew? (7)
27. Will old Scots music-hall king sounds exactly like a kingdom? (4)
28. "Scottish —— law" set up in the 16th century, (but not implemented until the 17th) to protect people against famine (4)

41

ACROSS

1. Steal from one half of Scottish shipyard? (4)
3. Contradict and revisit? (5–4)
9. Flowing to one side through Easter Inverness-shire? (4)
10. Redcap lark twittering in Glasgow zoo? (10)
12. Does the fact that it contains the largest volume of water make it monstrous? (4,4)
13. East Fife home? (6)
14. Where artists can cook nearby Edinburgh? (9, 5)
18. Change lead palm, then change again to discover where the finest specimens of pre-Reformation stained glass are to be found in Edinburgh (8, 6)
20. No Lucy — you mustn't act strangely! (6)
22. Neil begs around and gets heaps! (8)
24. Green clan insert right to be Argyllshire valley near Appin? (4, 6)
25. Can you see a young onion in a rosy border? (4)
26. Domestic fowl doubling as large boulders on the surface of the ground? (4–5)
27. Neat disarray causing sorrow? (4)

DOWN

1. Isle of Man race within regulation wood on the south side of the Beauly Firth? (6)
2. Invoice Ailsa for work done by a modern Scottish play- wright? (4,5)
4. Former Prime-minister happy to have his statue in the gardens of the British Legion's Douglas Haig Memorial Hall in Edinburgh? (9)
5. Stacks grain in blind streets? (4). . .
6. . . . and just the place to swop old farming jokes? (4–8)
7. Loiter in a port near Edinburgh, we hear? (5)
8. Little bell signified by murder done with jet group? (7)
11. Only Charlie seen about five in an Aberdeenshire fishing village? (12)
15. Care should be taken over rests and the girls ought to be confidential! (9)
16. Point rovin' eye over Southernwood? (9)
17. . . . and call into question a pine gum? (7)
19. Ancient ruined castle where Montrose stayed on the eve of the Battle of Alford sounds like "quiet"!(6)
21. Hooray for a seat? (5)
23. Looks like a famous Brazilian footballer with puncture! (4)

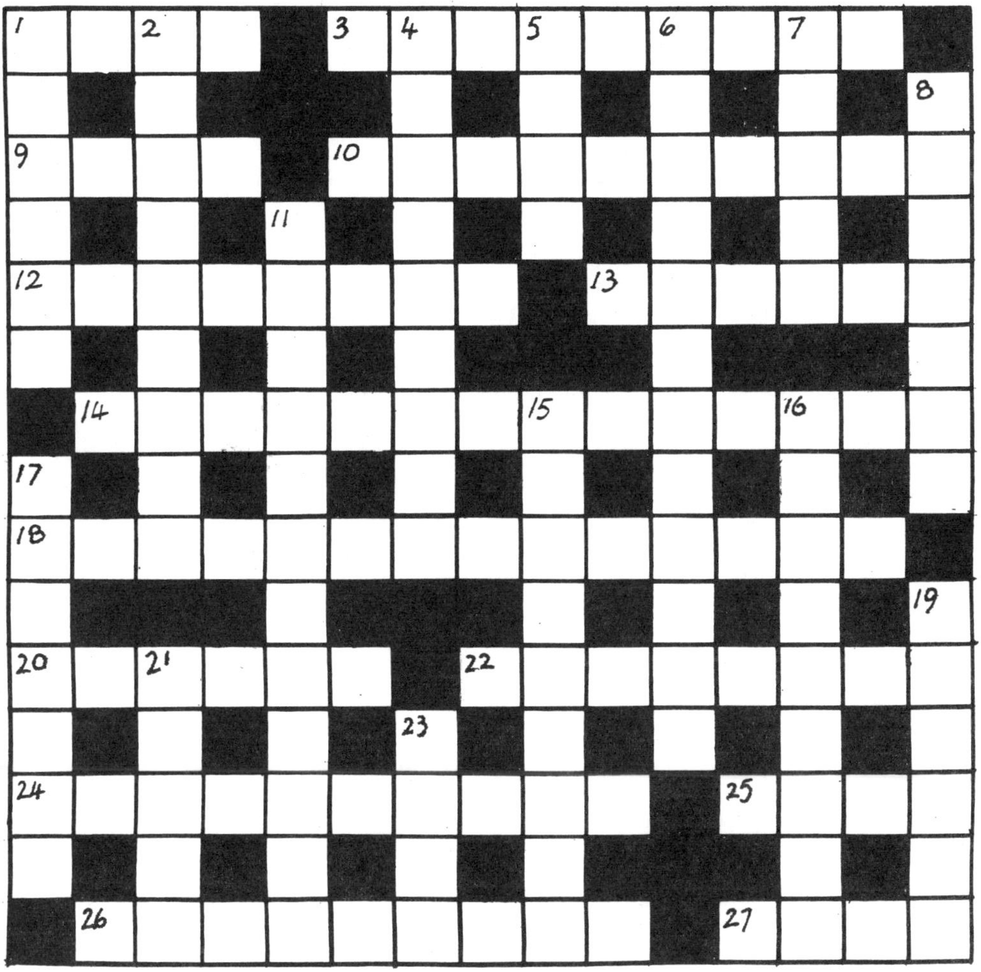
1
2
3
4
5
6
7
8
9
10
11
12
13
14
15
16
17
18
19
20
21
22
23
24
25
26
27

42

ACROSS

1. A little bit of Wiltshire presenting a hilly front to Edinburgh? (9, 5)
9. Shortened north-east Mediterranean and mixed potion having indicated pain? (5)
10. Trifle with red then spinster marries at long last, out of pride!(4–5)
11. Cuts sounds away from Scots novelist born in 1265? (4, 6)
12. Scots comedian Murray starts with artistic skill! (4)
14. Len Ewing? you'll find him in a disorderly state just outside Moray's county town! (3, 5)
16. Heavenly body and a five make up a highland peak! (6)
18. Did Burns say he only had Saturday night? (6)
19. American soldier and two Len's lost in small but picturesque Argyllshire valley? (4, 4)
21. Did Christina Rossetti hide in a castle in Mull? (4)
22. Is Heart of Midlothian often criticised here? (10)
25. "——— ——— Davie" famous Burns poem (7, 2)
26. You can see Italy or South Africa in this Arran glen! (5)
27. Recreational area of Edinburgh noted for its pond for model craft (10, 4)

DOWN

1. Stands me around church? It is one of the earliest known relics of Scottish Christianity (a cave with remains of walls) in Galloway (2, 6, 6)
2. Scots comedienne McLean has natural logarithm at each end it all adding up to a water-course running through Stormont near Dunkeld! (5)
3. Slider lies around complementing main cutlery? (4–6)
4. I'm sound about nothing – how extraordinary! (8)
5. Run Tay over peanut? (6)
6. Stole a flimsy wooden boat, we hear politely (4)
7. Sore hinge? put it right and get an unexpected present! (4–5)
8. Scene of more than two Falkirk battles? (10, 4)
13. Remain still beside it – his cure for feeling nauseated at food? (5–5)
15. A town is an arrangement for an Edinburgh former pupil! (9)
17. Iron bale melted down cardinal and first minister of Spain who arranged an abortive Scots rising against the English in 1719! (8)
20. Yokel gets confused when learner approaches and asks about northern river! (6)
23. Sort of a small island (with only one house) lying 15 miles south of Oban? (5)
24. You French with two points bite the dust? (4)

1
2
3
4
5
6
7
8
9
10
11
12
13
14
15
16
17
18
19
20
21
22
23
24
25
26
27

43

ACROSS

1. Teenager found just north of Glasgow? it's actually an expression for a woman over 36 (9, 5)
9. Mill casket up in part of Glasgow? (10)
10. Quiet! I'm to weed with a hoe! (4)
12. He returns in bad company but just wait! (5)
13. Five? four? late dual? it's all exactly the same (6)
16. Play at curling – that takes the biscuit (well most of it!) (4)
17. "——— ——— — Cuddy" short song composed by Robert Burns (3, 6, 1)
19. Rising pars? they are too coarse to be made into bread (4–6)
20. Dallas' state with bad ending finishing up as an island near Islay? (4)
22. His 'brae' is actually a glen leading down to Millport on Great Cumbrae! (6)
23. Take an interest in us – to begin with? (5)
26. Surprise shown inside company at shout in 'hide-and-seek'? (4)
27. Say it with a smile, fish is put on a frame for drying dairy product (6–4)
28. Novel asking for money on an agricultural area in the Crook of Devon, Fife? (10, 4)

DOWN

2. Munster contains northerly Shetland isle! (4)
3. Gabble around old, disused mill overlooking the great glen near Abriachan, Easter Inverness-shire? (6)
4. Former Archbishop of Canterbury's top now a leading Scottish publishing firm? (6, 4)
5. Treats harshly, railway gauge coming before heartless L.M.S.? (4)
6. Ensue hound being dead but not yet buried? (10)
7. Scottish senior football side's coil I can't shame? (8, 6)
8. Superb 14th century masterpiece written by John of Fordun purporting to be an anthology of the origins of the Scots (14)
11. 'Simple' saint who died on Gigha and was buried in Saddell Abbey in 1260? (5)
14. Former Prime Minister has exhibition added for triple-crown winning Scots rugby skipper! (6, 4)
15. Has enhance given us a lonely village in central Ross and Cromarty? (10)
18. Hog around morning spouting ancient Celtic alphabet? (5)
21. Compare fire flickering inside ancient historic Scots burgh?(6)
24. Can Hugh's nickname be used as a nudge?(4)
25. Damage, we hear, done to famous Troon college? (4)

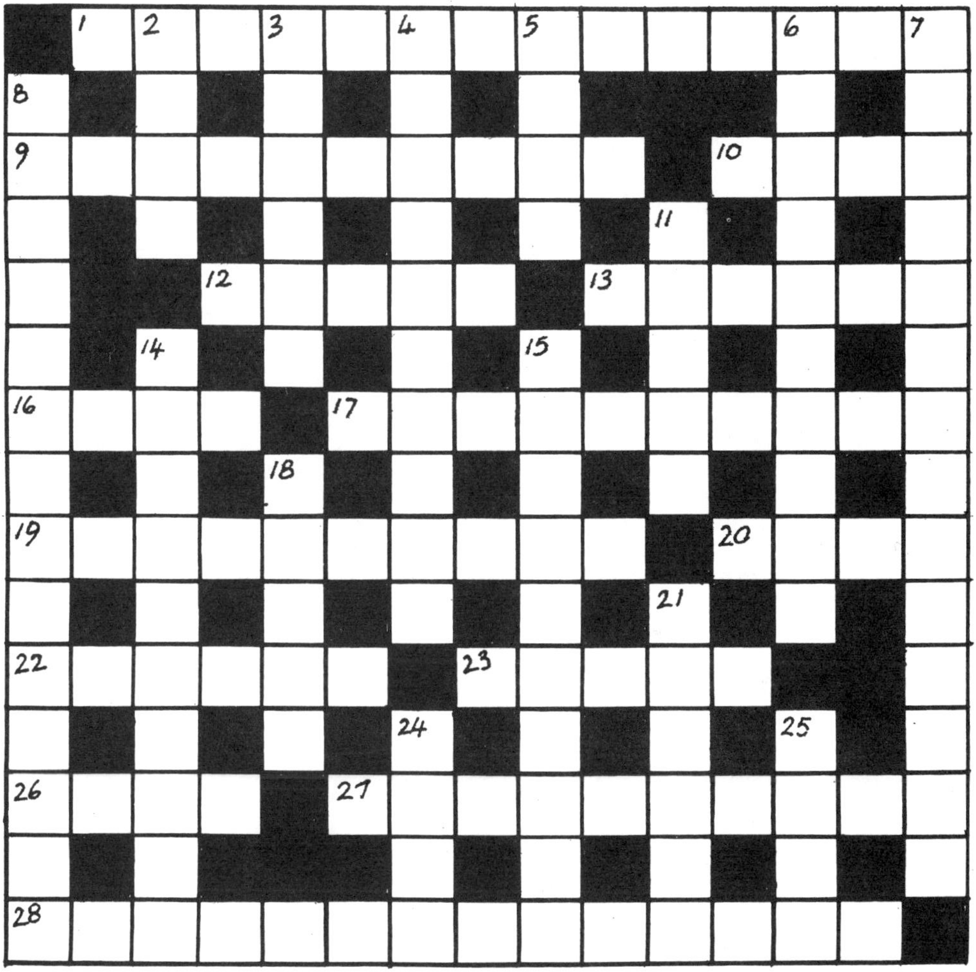

44

ACROSS

1. Our show of the ode was formerly at the Earl of Winton's Edinburgh home and is now the Scottish Naval, Military, and Air Force Veterans Residence! (10,5)
9. Dawson and Disney? a picturesque partnership near Stranraer? (7)

10, "—— Sowens" a Scottish dish made by steeping and fermenting the husks of oats in water then boiling (7)

11. Nora returns bringing a bunch of spotted orchids! (4)
12. Command given on the Glorious 12th? (5)
13. I win around a description of a confidant? (2, 2)
16. Formerly, shout about to tire? (7)
17. Medico and motoring organization express disapproval at being slow in movement! (7)
18. Hear odd assortment on the Isle of Bressay in the Shetlands? (7)
21. Swing or have a shivering fit? (7)
23. I rue over the great estate of the Viscounts Stonehaven near Fetteresso, Kincardineshire? (4)
24. Severe winds, we hear, inhabiting the Outer Hebrides? (5)
25. Bad habits stem from airts losing heart? (4)
28. The Spanish start cheating us near Hexham just over the Border? (7)
29. Lot Paul has to sort out to release surname of Alyth minister who spent 20 weeks in the Tower of London in 1651 because of his Covenanting beliefs! (7)
30. Title of a play performed for the first time at Cupar in 1525, written by Sir David Lindsay, the then Lyon King-of-Arms (3, 5, 7)

DOWN

1. One of the high-spots on a visit to Stirling perhaps? (7,8)
2. Show most in a short distance revealing a ruin in the Findhorn Glen, Nairnshire? (7)
3. It is equal to two under par, we hear! (4)
4. Fired better than projection of a building or castle wall? (7)
5. Answer the return made by a precept from chancery on an application for sasine (the act of giving legal possession)? (7)
6. Comedian who bobs up in a busy Glasgow street? (4) . . .
7. . . . and I quit Tory to give Aberdeen's main thoroughfare? (5, 2)
8. The auld enemy with us? it's only a children's game! (7, 3, 5)
14. A flannel nightcap? Hume fits it to a 'T'! (5)
15. Being cross, a son gets upset only having an English shilling? (5)
19. I raised motioning to ruined Fifeshire castle, home of David II where the great Scottish families had a meeting in 1335! (7)
20. Air duke in damp, wet weather? (7)
21. Slog over, Bridie makes you reach picturesque Sutherland coastal village! (7)
22. Art and French small bell? (7)
26. Thin liquid seen flowing through Dumfries? (4)
27. Bounce Strachan's head to small child? (4)

45

ACROSS

1. Wave-commanding English king exchanges first north for its last, constructing ship's cabin? (6)
4. Opposition to aparthied is big near Jedburgh? (5, 3)
10. Split at Berwick-upon-Tweed's seaside suburb? (7)
11. Fifeshire Bay has roulette dealer losing end without spin! (7)
12. Sod turning over new leaf? (4)
13. Wild broads removed to farming area situated around part of Hadrian's Wall! (10)
16. Was sorry about two rugby posts standing in a turf cut with grass adhering? (3–3)
17. Scottish goalkeeper gives old town importance? (7)
20. Fire found on some scale in south Ayrshire village? (7)
21. Absurd tales precede Roundhead with a hewn or highly polished stone? (6)
24. Lingers around north-north-east seeking the beautiful area around Dufftown in Banffshire (4,6)
25. Jura, for example lies off-shore! (4)
27. Glasgow holiday for blondes only? (3, 4)
29. The heart of the matter is always in the open! (7)
30. The close proximity of niggardliness? (8)
31. Raise rice about the street-head? (6)

DOWN

1. An old tax to cross a river between Kelso and Teviotdale? (8)
2. Famous old Edinburgh building, now a youth hostel, made from freezing rain, we hear? (6, 5)
3. Abstainers arrangement that is direct? (4)
5. Stretch of Ayrshire water you don't have to climb up to? (4, 4)
6. Peevish bingo call heard near Kilmarnock? (10)
7. A lick of the tongue at seeing a fair isle pattern? (3)
8. Manages successfully and is lewd, perverted? (6)
9. Royal winner can give you border river? (5)
14. Substantial part of Strathclyde is hilly and patrolled by heartless rangers? (11)
15. Banner in an alpine area near Arrochar? (3, 7)
18. Stable fodder-bins very handy for Noah's sore feet? (4–4)
19. After a vanishing act, Concord still remains! (8)
22. No togs, but dressed up Aberdeenshire family who, until its demolition in 1644, lived at Shethin Castle (6)
23. English county type found with a crook in Fife? (5)
26. Furrows return is harsh! (4)
28. Lady Rosebery's first, having chevalier at heart! (3)

1 2 3 4 5 6 7 8
9
10 11
12 13 14
15
16 17
18 19
20 21
22 23
24 25
26
27 28 29
30 31

46

ACROSS

1. Peer and first director–general of the B.B.C. who died in his 82nd year in 1971 (4, 5)
6. Pa gets mixed up with spy and becomes sodden! (5)
9. Surname of Edinburgh born scientist who gave his name to a 'prism' used in polarising light (5)
10. Golden tin re-opened revealing a kind of apple? (9)
11. Talk at length on the source of ham holding a jar of cream! (4, 3)
12. European nation laying claim to bay near Stromness in the Orkneys? (7)
14. He's Rutland bound – starting his journey from old scots county! (10)
15. It's bottled up somewhere between Alloa and Stirling! (4)
18. One of the Inner Hebrides with strong religious connections, a monastery having been built there in A.D. 563! (4)
19. Slew Lallan sprinting hero? (5, 5)
23. Nave not excavated in village near Dingwall? (7)
25. Support meal not taken by guests at a table? (4–3)
26. Rattle and nit about Fifeshire village! (9)
27. She is upset by terminations! (5)
28. I rent out and farm pig nut! (5)
29. Neil Munro's captain of a vital spark! (4, 5)

DOWN

1. Shrink a real crazy old Scottish county! (11)
2. Former estate in Midlothian which was used as the site of the new Heriot-Watt University (9)
3. Err and leaps about to fall into scandalous sin? (8)
4. Gill of ale? that's an unlawful thing! (7)
5. Old emperor who went to the wall before he reached Scotland? (7)
6. Contralto formerly at Clydebank? (6)
7. Tap up North America in Ayrshire village? (5)
8. That which shows sign of fatigue, we hear? (3)
13. Local name for the old Roman Road which runs from Edinburgh to Ayr via Rutherglen (5, 6)
16. Spin latch around and bedaub! (9)
17. Sh! Willis is whirling around! (8)
20. Pan gill – upset and in a fit of sulking! (7)
21. Tea-ware reassembled holding liquid near Moffat in Dumfriesshire? (2, 5)
22. Stroke made in exact observance of the rules! (6)
24. Crazy! A 'Tony' being awarded to Berwickshire village! (5)
26. Many are rebuilt as a cattle enclosure! (4)

1
2
3
4
5
6
7
8
9
10
11
12
13
14
15
16
17
18
19
20
21
22
23
24
25
26
27
28
29

47

ACROSS

3. Famous part of Edinburgh in tall loch? (6,4)
8. A valley or plain through which a river runs in east Rathlin Island? (6)
9. Lord Home's handle? (4)
10. Kidnapped author gets time but escapes to Ayrshire industrial burgh? (10)
11. The poultry farmer's wife? (3)
13. School loses early combine and is given a shovel! (4)
14. Seabird? a Scots one makes East Lothian golfing resort! (7)
15. Sore point? points exchanged for historic Ayrshire village! (4)
17. Famous economist, brought up in Kirkcaldy, could be either black or gold! (5)
20. I drew around the troublesome! (5)
22. Five hundred and one add postscript to fluids which kill sheep-vermin? (4)
24. Dart around Ron in this Shetland isle? (7)
25. Travelled for nothing or around nothing? (4)
27. Are about the Lord Advocate who persuaded Hare to turn King's evidence against Burke? (3)
28. MacBeth's predecessor (4,6)
29. Call a horse to come near and give weather forecast? (4)
30. Publish about a hybrid breed? (6)
31. William the Conqueror's rule being held high near the banks of the Firth of Tay? (7,3)

DOWN

1. Tailors nickname is what the surgeon is called to do to his patients after operation, we hear! (8)
2. Ravel'd then unravelled lace-making Ayrshire burgh? (6)
3. Can hods be rebuilt to give the duke who was the founder of the first chair of medicine at St.Andrews University? (7)
4. The French hit out at eastern port near Edinburgh? (5) ...
5. ... but nothing to hinder the west coast equivalent? (4)
6. A small distance for a coat to become a rocky shipping hazard to those entering the Firths of Forth and Tay? (8)
7. Extend overdraft to chief in order to develop Midlothian town? (8)
12. What was to be given to them with a hundred pipers? (4)
14. Pang returns straight away to taunt! (4)
16. A sod of a bay rebuilt on Loch Fyne? (4)
17. Sent tarn out to Celtic missionary who is thought to have founded a religious colony at Banchory in the 5th century? (2,6)
18. River one has to cross to obtain metallic ore? (4-4)
19. Treasure an essential in seeking Ospreys for example? (4)
21. A doer-die? conceals an Abbot of the 8th century who has a marvellously preserved slab on show in the Museum of Antiquities, Edinburgh (8)
23. Scottish guillemot begins with slip towards upturned wad? (7)
25. Piece of fish with an attempt to be in 4 Scottish places at one time — and succeeding! (6)
26. Former New Zealand athlete recorded the same as Scots' Sharp? (5)...
28. ... and sharp, we hear, English 18th century actor who retired to Rothesay! (4)

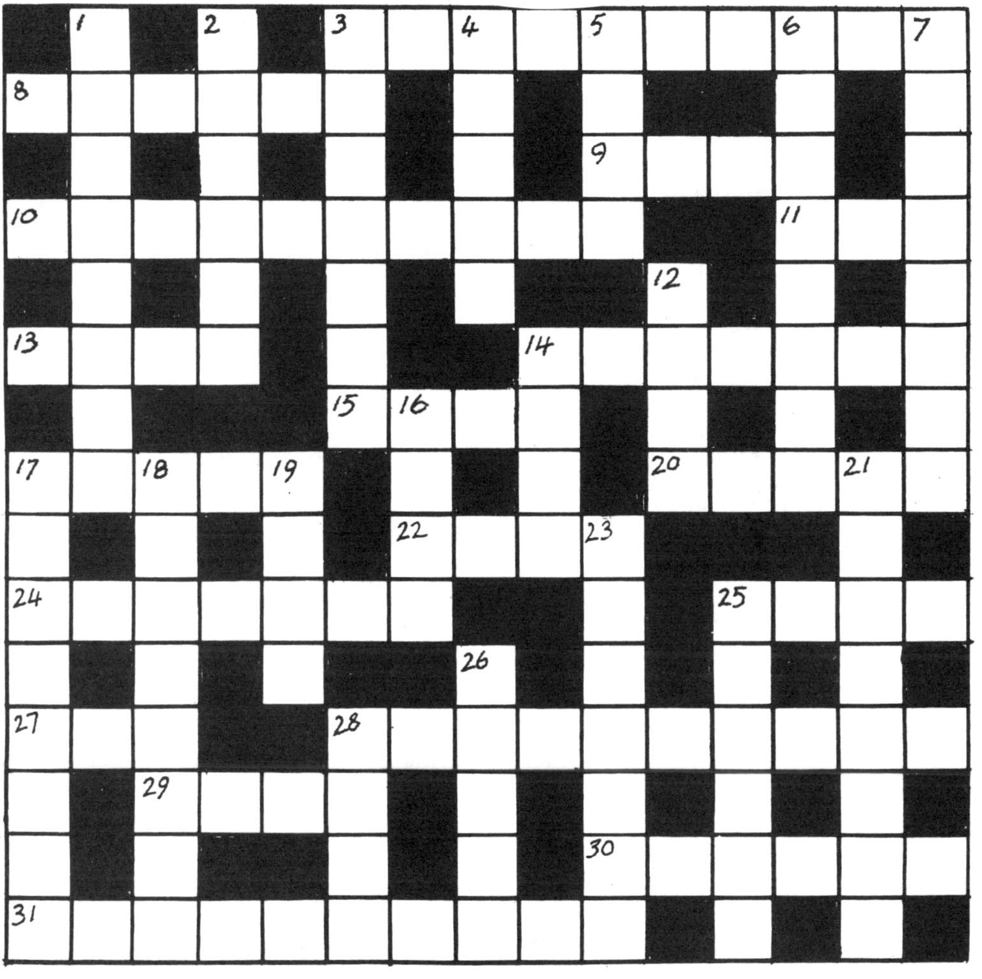

48

ACROSS

1. American violinist comes to the old Edinburgh approach road? (4, 3)
5. Piece of fish becomes essential part of execution? (4–3)
9. Ken is confused about the dagger (5)
10. Embrace Spaniard inside, being castle and ancient home of the McCullochs near Gatehouse-of-Fleet? (9)
11. Dress barley by having little saint on top of haystack? (6)
12. Being very nearly English could he be called an outsider (8)
14. Another rising? it's only an upward break in a mineral stratum! (5)
15. Meet wi' oor famous distillery outside Keith? (9)
18. Mr. Wells runs into dunt and becomes ancient fort on North Bute! (9)
20. Monster loses her head on nearing east Aberdeenshire village? (5)
22. Too much bending and bells ringing can cause unsightly swellings! (7)
24. Deceives by mixing-up keys after pointing in the direction of Stranraer? (6)
26. Milk-sac wedged between two streets (one in reverse) giving grassy patches on hillsides? (9)
27. Does Luncarty lie in slice of land? no quite the opposite! (5)
28. Surname of the Anstruther-born poet whose major work "Anster Fair" was published in 1812 (7)
29. Neither partner secure in the highlands? (7)

DOWN

1. N.A.T.O. in good order? – broadcasting in the Ayrshire area! (4–5)
2. Border water caused by a cut in oil platform? (7)
3. Lad's lobster pot can become an awe-inspiring N.W. mountain near Skye (3, 6)
4. Old Scots burgh you can hold a candle to? (4)
5. The little weight ratio which was formulated at this university? (6–4)
6. Among it the Perthshire river loses Lochhead? (5)
7. A goodbye can bring happiness to the first two instalments of promissory note! (7)
8. Enticer has to resit in return! (5)
13. She has a convent in Bruntsfield and hope in Rosyth! (2, 8)
16. Can sheep-dip become a beautiful Dumfriesshire valley and then run into the Esk? (4, 5)
17. Former Prime Minister's cap holder can turn into the Manor-house at Pitlochrie and be the site of an old Roman camp! (9)
19. A modern fireplace standing on Largo Bay, Fife? (7)
21. Sad, kilt standing all alone in the Atlantic? (2, 5)
22. Become ready for race? (5)
23. Insulin diagnosed as being rubber? (5)
25. Sauna loses a part lying around Montrose? (4)

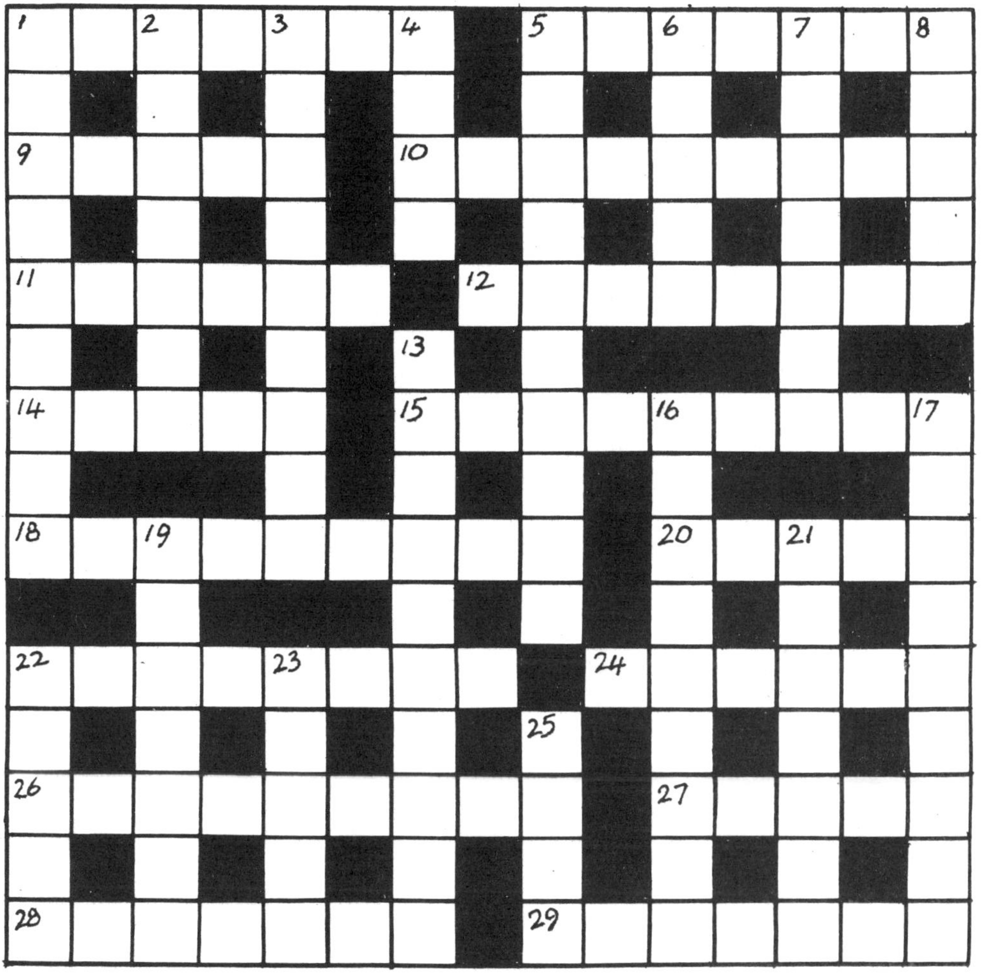
1
2
3
4
5
6
7
8
9
10
11
12
13
14
15
16
17
18
19
20
21
22
23
24
25
26
27
28
29

49

ACROSS

1. My French? I join post to establish Fife village near Cupar! (8)
5. Large part of Deeside has a young man following the North-east? (6)
9. Border abbey town with no liquid? (8)
10. Ring excited — then smash to powder! (4,2)
12. A lean star can be seen to be the R.A.F. Rest Centre near Tarland in Argyllshire! (9)
14. A denim, mohair blanket might reveal the surname of the friend of Mrs McLehose (Clarinda) who did much to assist her affair with Robert Burns! (5)
15. Surname of the much loved Scots comedy actor famous for his portrayal of the Schoolmistress of St.Trinians. (3)
16. And paid for a sheep-pen? (6)
19. Once a can squeezed between the same two points? (5)
22. Can one bruise strike with shame? (5)
23. Holy man and ne'er-do-well combine to give a roll of flax ready for processing! (6)
25. The same name — as in Castlemilk? (3)
28. That is returning between three learners giving a single stitch in markin on a piece of embroidery! (7)
29. I hitch Ken to a rocky islet lying in the Forth? (9)
32. Child with neckpiece can be snug and warm ! (6)
33. Part of Glasgow where you can find a thistle? (8)
34. Wonner about looking for fame? (6)
35. Les Green — crazy, idle lounger! (8)

DOWN

1. Could this be the Indian quarter of St.Andrews? (6)
2. Horse talk? — speak on a refusal (3-3)...
3. ... and horse found on the Oliphant farm where Burns lived from 1766? (5)
4. "Auld baudrans by the — sits, an wi' her loof her face a-washin,"(Robert Burns: Willie Wastle) (5)
6. 'Humble' journalist who is rugby expert and top councillor? (5,4)
7. Yet naming can create a state of great excitement! (8)
8. The searcher and traveller could have been the name of the Aberdeen-based ocean-going research vessel? (8)
11. A fair mock-heroic poem written and published in 1812 by William Tennant? (6)
13. A little stick of rhubarb in Dunbartonshire? (3)
17. Live chow I arrange to meet at a senior football park? (9)
18. Enquire within, gin being made from a rough, green gooseberry? (6)
20. After dance, tear up to picturesque Deeside burgh? (8)
21. Scottish burgh seen on the front of a US $10 bill? (8)
24. Plant a tree in Isla's hills? (3)
26. Trouble could be caused if backing into ruler! (6)
27. Crown with hole in the middle, fit for a double chin? (6)
30. A hundred get the bird and go to live in Fife? (5)
31. A large straw basket,for carrying door-openers by the sound of it! (5)

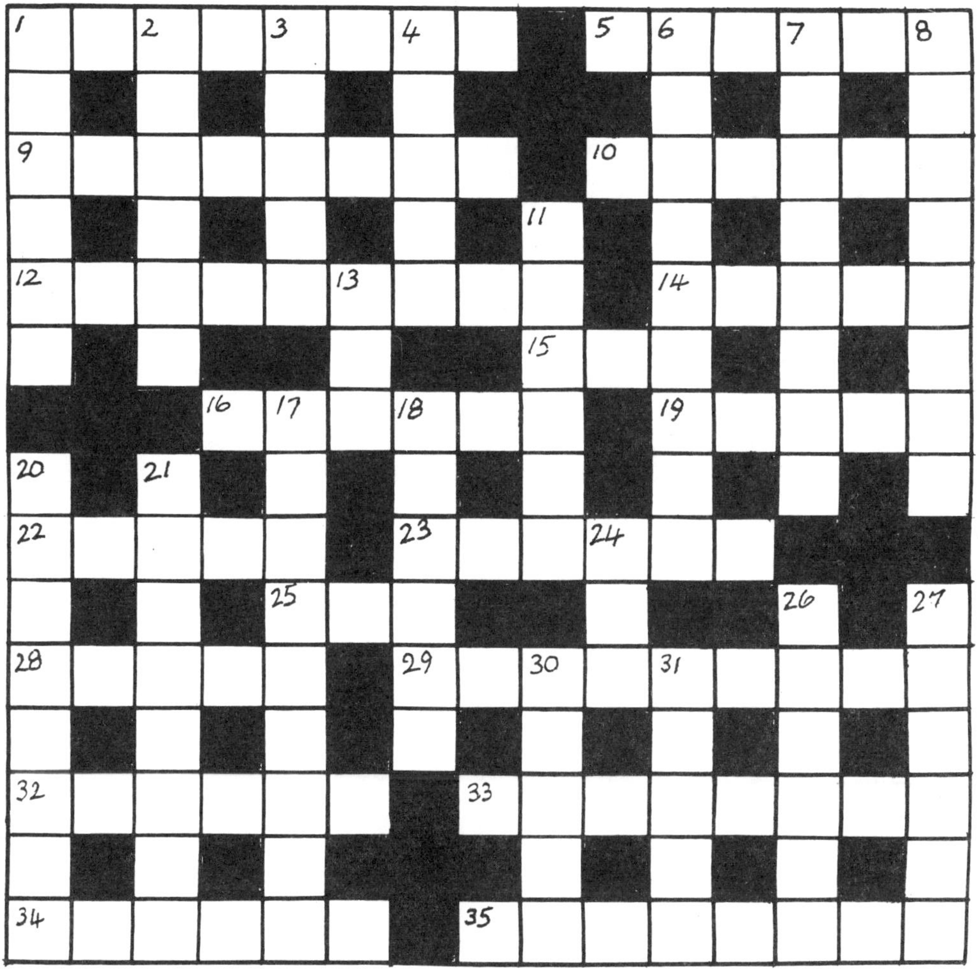

50

ACROSS

1. Scottish safeblower who was the subject of a controversial report by Lord Hunter (5, 6)
9. Scottish Queen who was executed in 1587 (4)
10. Check on huge escarpment on the English side of the Cheviots? (11)
11. American soldier caught in the middle of Aberdeenshire river surrounded by unionist and English! (4)
14. Racehorses who normally follow whiskies? (7)
17. A dull arrangement having a Shetland law of succession? (5)
18. Mrs. Thatcher loses her composure in driving a nail loosely? (5)
19. Church of Scotland officer of the more adult kind? (5)
20. Seen returning from the east with a sneeze? (5)
21. Being in love Ramsay is above everything? (4, 1)
22. Is the mixture to be straightened out to give legal compensation? (5)
23. Only a very short distance from Huntly by the sound of it! (5)
24. Riles at being upset by a strainer for milk? (5)
25. Try hats around north coast village near Thurso? (7)
29. Teach about a mad Earl? (4)
32. Drown near an orderly pier in Loch Lomond, handy for climbing Ben Lomond? (11)
33. The ridge of roof sounds just like the back of the neck! (4)
34. New furniture? hardly, when it's an old colloquial phrase for the Court of Session! (5, 6)

DOWN

2. Stirlingshire river flowing through Stratford? (4)
3. Village of West Morayshire with a good wall? (4)
4. A thousand move gradually forward until lying between the Hebrides and the mainland? (5)
5. Being never at odds, suggests a suitable person to marry? (5)
6. I rage about grain dried in a pot before being ground in a hand-mill? (5)
7. Grew small to become the "better half" of a famous Scottish athletic team? (6, 5)
8. Cowshed stage founded in 1933 in St. Andrews? (4, 7)
12. Fired on Arran, say? then move across to stand on the Fifeshire coast? (11)
13. Bird's neck – full of steel in Motherwell? (11)
14. Less Ché repeats any old tale? (7)
15. Each, for short, pass away to leave the M.P. for Midlothian? (5)
16. Sour – in pig-pen, creating a squabble? (7) . . .
19. . . . and fester 'ere about abstainer? (5)
26. Your Scandinavian god of thunder consumes duck! (5) . . .
27. . . . sole reason for a gala ne'erday? (5)
28. Persist in being tricked in that place? (3, 2)
30. A shoemaker outlaws in return? (4)
31. Having health, laugh with the French? (4)

51

ACROSS

1. Tap shoe in Lanarkshire village? (8)
5. Tea within an old Scottish village near Loch Tay? (6)
9. Peebles castle sounds as if it may require walkway? (8)
10. Does a branch and the early dawn combine to create a cake of manure and coal-dust used as a fuel? (6)
11. A head east-coast port? two bits of it are! (8)
12. We row. I am anxious to get it past! (4, 2)
14. Teach Allan to climb near Ullapool (2, 8) . . .
18. . . . and dig a murder up near Alyth in Perthshire! (5, 5)
22. Its 'strength' lies in being earthworks near the border at Hawick! (6)
23. Oy Nessie! excusing yourself for absence from a law court! (8)
24. Stane about a hundred and puts oneself under a legal obligation! (6)
25. The chemist has a collection! (8)
26. Thus a ruler is guaranteeing! (6)
27. Lang lies about being the western most valley in Angus? (8)

DOWN

1, 2. Brown a numbered box? sounds like the home of this eleven! (6, 6)

3. Hat not there, so drink to the very bottom of the glass? (3, 3)
4. Treat sound opponent? (10)
6. Worm cell constructed and built the old fort at Ayr? (8)
7. Tree person who used to administer the old Scottish burghs? (8)
8. What is needed when the bulb is burst is liberal and progressive in doctrine! (3, 5)
13. Line probes around north-west highland peak? (3, 7)
15. Lauder's leader repeats and arranges to become landowners under the Shetland Laws of Succession! (8)
16. Bound to lose Orkney's capital and dismiss fiancé? (4–4)
17. Bent mole hiding out in an English border village? (8)
19. Kilmarnock carpet family formerly playing premier league football? (6)
20. Being sly, three different directions must be followed to reach point near Scapa Flow? (6)
21. We bank and are attached to side of workshop? (4, 2)

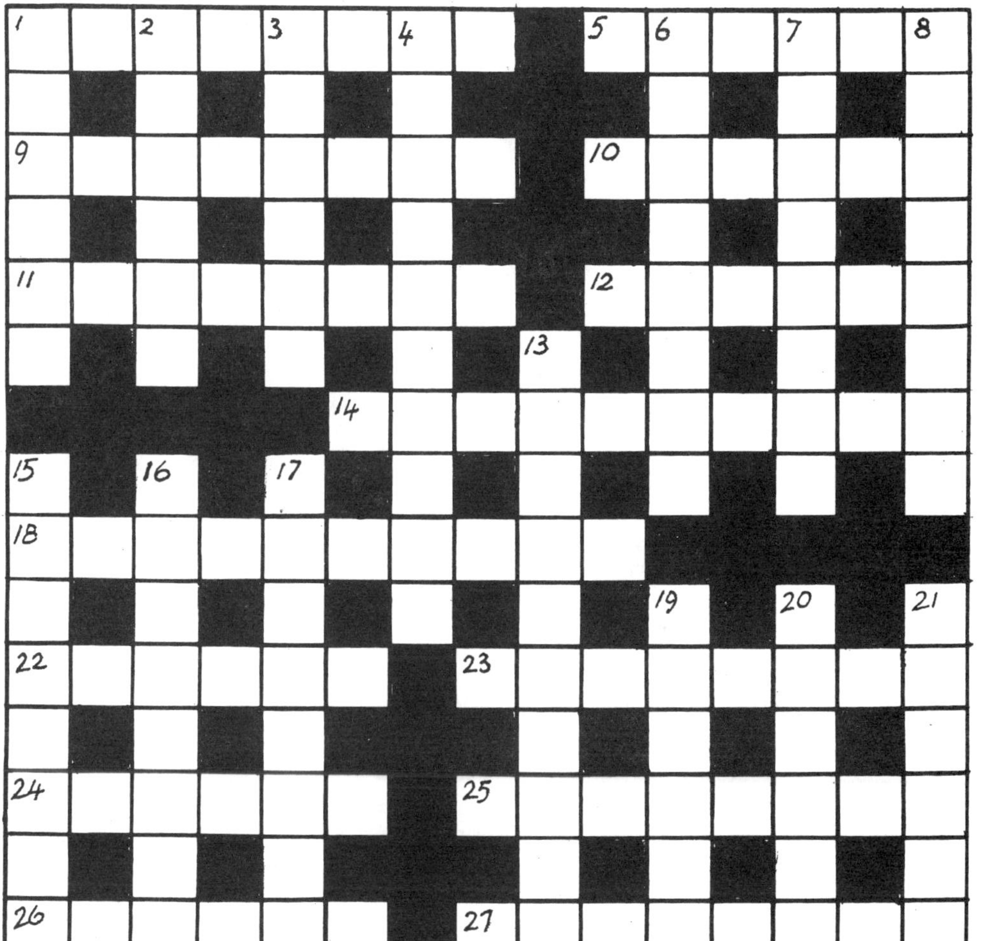
1
2
3
4
5
6
7
8
9
10
11
12
13
14
15
16
17
18
19
20
21
22
23
24
25
26
27

52

ACROSS

1. The motley crew who were Scotlands most successful ice-hockey side of the 1950's and '60's? (7, 7)
9. Clever at eating a quick meal? (6)
10. Eke salad out of a picturesque wooded area on the south bank of the River Beauly in Inverness-shire? (8)
11. Animals introduced in 1899 are skied about Loch Ness-side? (4, 4)
13. Former Scottish football manager who couldn't wait for Mondays? (6)
14. Point to the little Ibrox player? he is moving gradually to one side! (4)
15. North-west loch painted often with a broad brush? (5)
16. Low learner attached to a slipper? (4)
17. Pitch cricketer would like to see in Easter Ross? (6)
19. Instrument sweet as part of the Treshnish Isles off the Argyllshire coast? (4, 4)
21. Increases grease around horse? (8)
23. Add a cat to this clergyman to create fireside pastime played with a stick made red in the fire and passed around? (5)
24. Looting present? then occupying the seat in church set aside for public rebuke! (9, 5)

DOWN

1. Mrs. Thatcher doing U-turns? it's only a daddy-longlegs! (8, 6)
2. Is clan Irish? reorganized in time to become the family name of the Earls of Orkney (8)
3. Shout inside to disorganized Celt, about to have a hard and heavy fall! (6)
4. Sounds like an Orkney island has good current connection? (4)
5. Milk cork shaken up near Stranraer? (8)
6. Challenge the speechless without end and cause uproar! (6)
8. Clint Easte? long ruined near Kilwinning! (8, 6)
12. Choir boy former skipper of Derby County and Scotland? (5)
15. Industrial Lothians town for wash door? (8)
16. Surname of the Scots-born authoress whose most famous work is the touching love story "The Gowk Storm" (8)
18. The musical description of the Rocks of Aden? (6)
20. Replace the Rest and Be Thankful? (6)
22. Yes north can become third member of the Auld-Lang partnership! (4)

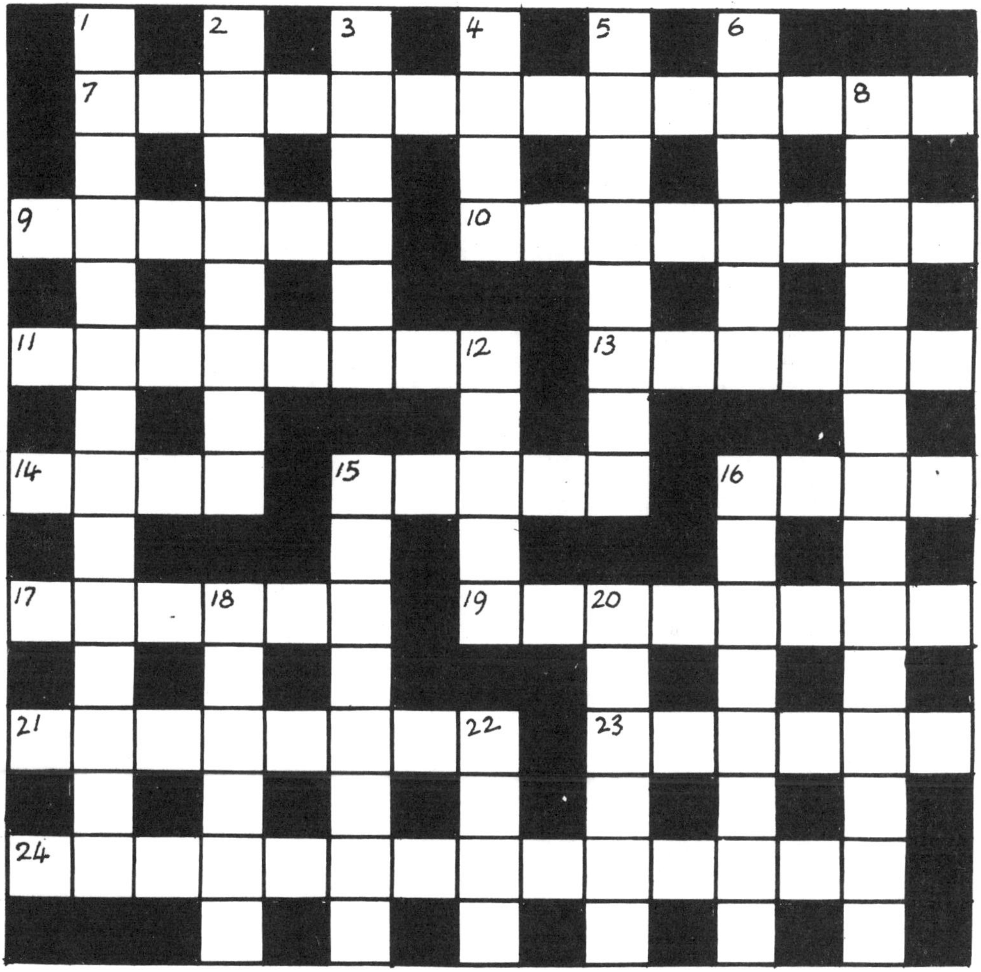
1 2 3 4 5 6
7 8
9 10
11 12 13
14 15 16
17 18 19 20
21 22 23
24

53

ACROSS

1. A five star arrangement with view of Argyllshire peak! (6)
5. Veto – it is thrown out into the river at Hawick! (6)
8. Yon little Irish upstart is as hard as metal to the Scots! (5)
9. Liverpool-born musician who became gardiner professor of music at Glasgow University in 1966 (6)
10. A twister of a Scots poet, perhaps? (6)
11. A young salmon will crawl mostly with change of head! (5)
14. 'Magic' name for old Yester Castle? (6, 2)
16. Surname of the Texan golfer who came to Royal Troon in 1982 to defend the British Open Championship (6)
18. Uppish group perhaps, formed to promote Scotland overseas? (8, 7)
20. F.T. safe? quit it! (3–3)
22. Renfrewshire burgh literally lost in the North-east! (8)

25, 27. Could this senior Scottish football side also be playing 'starkers'? (5, 6)

28. Re-read about industrialized Ayrshire village? (6)
29. The same direction shown three times by motoring organization to border burgh? (5)
30. Really crazy part of Argyllshire near St. Columba's cave! (6)
31. Scottish Earldom found in a place of worship? (6)

DOWN

1. Go with spur contraption for a sparrow? (6)
2. "Stand to your —— and march in good order, . . ." (Scottish traditional song: Blue Bonnets o'er the Border) (4)
3. American state in which lies the port of Cape Breton, where, in 1695, a 'Scottish Colonial Scheme' was set up for trade with the Indies and Africa (8)
4. It's St. Andrews H.Q. governs birdies! (5, 3, 7)
5. Let try upset the Scottish brothers who led a Scottish 'folk' literature movement in the 18th century! (6)
6. Particle article – it's in the Inner Hebrides! (4)
7. Famous Caithness glass designer sounding like a row of houses! (6)
12. Scottish mistletoe – a panacea? (3–4)
13. "Lord, hear my earnest cry and pray'r
—— that Presbyt'ry of Ayr!" (Burns: Holy Willie's Prayer) (7)
15. Scots mind over a duck and spruce, perhaps! (5) . . .
17. Hot air I leave behind in Midlothian village! (5)
19. Ivory animal, sounding remarkably like 19th century Scottish novelist! (8)
20. Give Grampian Regional Council leader an apology, we hear? (6)
21. Scots deny – so to speak? (6)
23. The lady belonging to a hundred pipers! (6)
24. "Wee modest, crimson tipp't flower, thou's met me in an —— hour" (Burns: To A Mountain Daisy) (4)
26. Constant point politician has to make about 16th century Scottish Psalter composer? (4)

54

ACROSS

1. Popular Kilmarnock crook that is a Perthshire battleground! (13)
10. Entrances to the Scot's intestines? (7)
11. Container used for many a Scottish export! (4–3)
12. Raw foggy wind which requires head covering, we hear! (4)
13. Ayr in a turmoil after visit by Princess of Wales? – Boswell would have recorded it here! (5)
14. Internationally it's sung by Auld and Lang! (4)
17. Area of Argyllshire, scene of an infamous slaughter of the MacDonald clan in 1692 (4, 3)
18. Above gratitude – that's this part of Kilmarnock! (7)
19. Annoying remark made after spill down west Perthshire glen? (7)
22. Blend that is mixed on the "Mountain of God" in Perthshire? (3, 4)
24. In Easter Ross the fertile part of John Logie Baird? (4)
25. Lay two pounds about the famous Angus family! (5)
26. Scottish Football Association in mix-up in front of rugby post? – trouble! (4)
29. S. Voe – early terminal experiencing trouble with tenants' right to necessary materials! (7)
30. Haystacker, perhaps, who helped Telford plan the Caledonian Canal! (7)
31. Religiously measure building to see if fit for royal garden parties in Edinburgh? (13)

DOWN

2. Must we have ungrateful Scots tearing up? (7)
3. Selkirk-born author who has no short comings? (4)
4. With a little hesitation hide the point of Clyde bridge? (7)
5. "Don ——" the nom-de-plume of Scots author and nationalist R.B. Cunninghame Graham (7)
6. The Scottish vegetable to tide you over, – so to speak! (4)
7. Chin up on Ayr United playing in Tay village? (7)
8. Knighted Scottish businessman who recently rebuilt his interest in large department stores (3, 4, 6)
9. Right! Even I ink over Fife industrial town! (13)
15. Old Scots wooden drinking vessel holding squirt! (5)
16. The destiny of Scotland beneath the English throne! (5)
20. Musselburgh public school to let or knock down? (7)
21. We hear a cry, a concoction of dried grass and boiling water! (3–4)
22. The Scottish saint who died in north Berwick in 606 A.D. had no hair and was a communist! (7)
23. Italian scholar and teacher who taught the sons of James IV and whose influence was seen in the formation of Aberdeen University (7)
27. Ivy about Robert's head – having the right to play her marble from any position! (4)
28. "—— Stone" in Scotland, a hard black stone full of holes which makes reverberating noises (4)

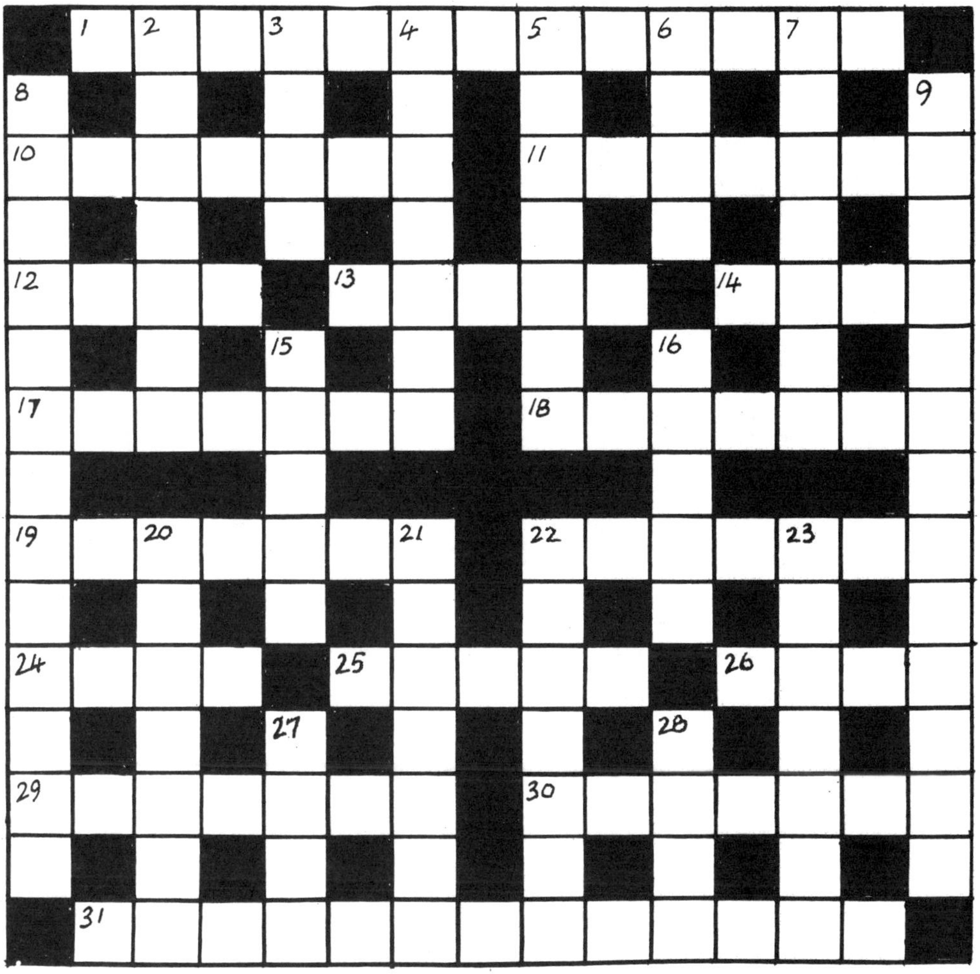

55

ACROSS

1. Dick goes round the outside to sell drink from up-turned van to famous 18th century house in Glen Dubh, Argyllshire! (10)
6. Sail up an Angus river? (4)
9. Varying, err on the side of Loch Lochy village! (10)
10. Brilliant start for a wish-bone? (4)
12. Name of the Bellshill-born singer who has achieved international stardom as a result of her appearance on the TV programme "The Big Time" (6, 6)
15. The blonde girl Burns wrote a love poem to? (4, 5)
17. Famous Scottish painter, with re-designed chore? (5)
18. Enough Scots round a penny! – it's given at weddings! (5)
19. Togle Lorn strangely wore in beautiful area near Gatehouse-of-Fleet? (4,5)
20. Title initial and name of the luckless leader of the English cavalry at Bannockburn (3, 1, 8)
24. Dug up nave and discovered the water joining the Dee at Banchory! (4)
25. Takes it on the chin, faints, and comes up with little Mull village! (2, 8)
26. Put question to force – what is this village? Gaelic for 'a tailing ridge'! (4)
27. Small distance I break up to ruined Graham Castle near Aberuthven, Perthshire? (10)

DOWN

1. "The ——'s Awa Wi' The Exciseman" short song by Burns reflecting his time as a customs officer (4)
2. Tomintoul valley overlooking island off the coast of Mull? (4)
3. East coast burgh and tourist resort which housed the infamous 'witch-trials' of 1591 involving King James VI (5, 7)
4. The east gave up making a Scottish journey! (5)
5. Motor along a valley to Kintyre village? (9) . . .
7. . . . and a river valley gets the bird, we hear, near Applecross in the west highlands! (6, 4)
8. The Scottish sprinter who struck gold at the Moscow Olympics in 1980! (5, 5)
11. Scottie's ancestor, so we're told! (5, 7)
13. Stane graft needed to cure hangover? (10)
14. The biblical desert standing on the western extremity of the Isle of Mull? (10)
16. No listing required for Royal Highland Show? (9)
21. Fit H.R. into a Scottish wood? (5)
22. Chess term, we hear in wheeltrack! (4)
23. King James VI's wife from Denmark! (4)

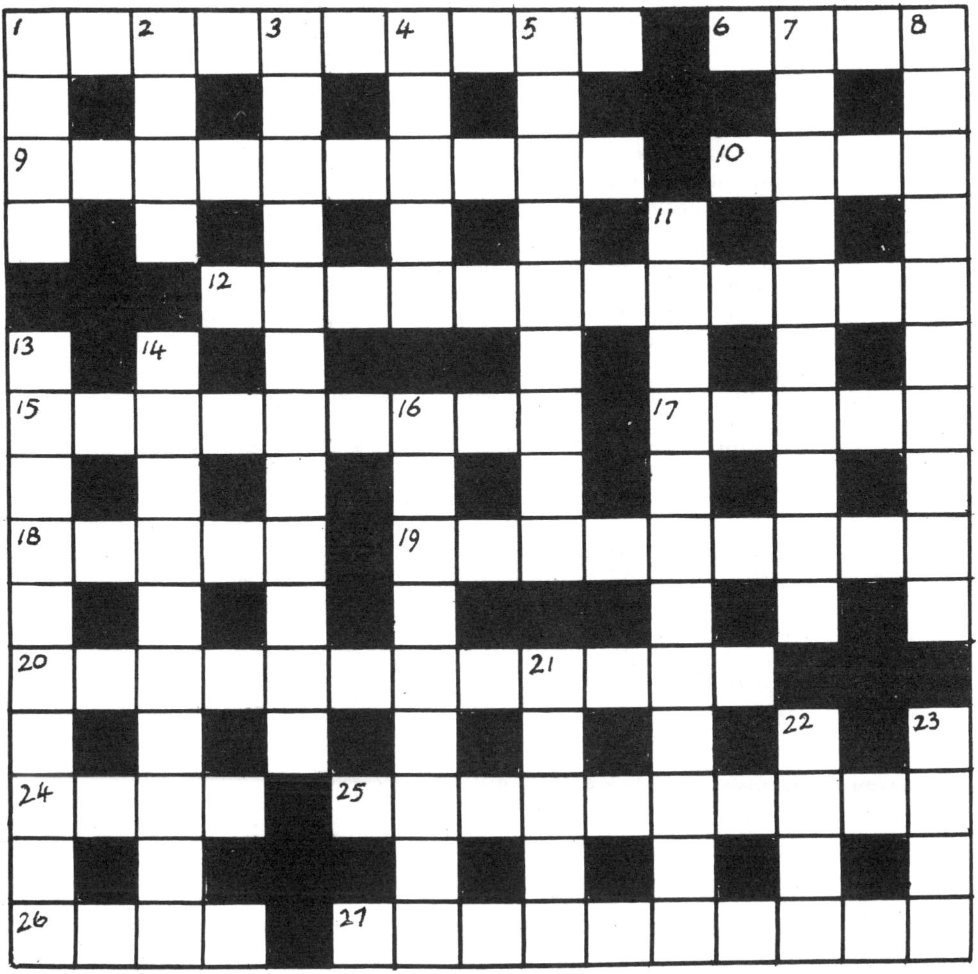

56

ACROSS

1, 10. Great Scottish waterway built by Thomas Telford and opened in 1803 (10, 5)
6. "—— Bheinn" peak on Islay rising to 1544 ft. (4)
10. See 1.
11. American harbour in other words forming one end of Carnoustie? (4, 5)
12. Lager may change into main ingredient of porridge! (8)
13. Old Scots grandmother coming from some place between Annan and Nairn? (5)
15. Held Rod up and became funny walker! (7)
17. Angle changing very softly in Galloway Valley? (4, 3)
19, 28. Sports ground of Edinburgh Academy, scene of the first England v. Scotland rugby match in 1871 (7, 5)
21. With southern, they're down in the borders! (far from it) (7)
22. North Ayrshire town he bit off! (5)
24. 'Cert' any number can back at this Glasgow Stadium? (8)
27. Bonie 'tic? I support them with an early christian! (9)
28. See 19.
29. Lead given to north Berwick family related to R.L. Stevenson? (4)
30. The tenners paid up to visit loch and priory near Montrose? (10)

DOWN

1. Curling 'tee' found on a poultry farm? (4)
2. Yearn for highlands, being in West Lothian village? (9)
3. Crazy lady right in the middle of Ayrshire town? (5)
4. The time we yearn about in Scotland! (3, 4)
5. A glass I break after a toast to the stormy petrel! (7)
7. Departing, we hear, from historic loch? (5)
8. It provides a cover for 'The Broons'! (6, 4)
9. Does old Scottish peer, nearly 100 years old, have only one good leg? (8)
14. The Scots' opposition to the long loaf? (10)
16. "——rain" Scottish term used for rain coming from the south-west, usually with a clear sky-line (8)
18. A land nane upset – a peerage title of Robert the Bruce! (9)
20. Nice, hot mixture given to a puny Scot? (7)
21. The Scots word for a golf-club which has its head set at almost 90° to the shaft (7)
23. Afraid illegal statement hides Aberdeen official commemorated in magnificent stain-glass window in the cathedral church there! (5)
25. A lot of printing – the kind of 'job' Scots say is dangerous to health! (5)
26. Puff and pant after catching fish without heart? (4)

57

ACROSS

1. Senior Scottish football team "ready" to play? (7, 7)
9. Fulton's handle? a born comedian! (5)
10. Old, ruined church in Alyth, Argyllshire whose aisle is known locally as "The Arches" (2, 7)
11. Muddler Lom mixed up in Aberdeenshire burgh! (10)
12. Father joining University of Wales? it must be a Scots trick! (4)
14. Christian missionary to whom the first Royal Church at Crathie, Aberdeenshire, was dedicated (2, 6)
16. "—— ale" old Scots tradition of giving alcohol to the workforce upon completion of a building (6)
18. Tell the story of a Kintyre late-wake? (6)
19. "The Auld ——" the popular name given in Scotland, to the Détante which existed with France between 1296 and 1560 (8)
21. Nairnshire village in which a hundred joined Rob's partner? (4)
22. Royal regiment formed in 1681 from an earlier body of Dragoon Guards (5, 5)
25. Lemon a lad squeezes out on the mid-and-west Lothian boundary valley! (9)
26. "—— —— win" Scottish sailing term to denote a good winnowing breeze (4, 1)
27. Scottish poet and playwright who was born a cripple in Anstruther in 1784, his most famous work being 'Anster Fair' (7, 7)

DOWN

1. Noo grand charts needs alteration for Aberdeen F.C.'s schemer! (6, 8)
2. Enquired about Scot publishing the marriage banns? (5)
3. Old Scottish 21/- bill sung in West Africa? (6, 4)
4. Was third! – no use to old Scots miners? (4–4)
5. Bonnie Jean needing protection from Burns? (6)
6. Young American lady visiting Tarbert initially names Scots-born biographer of Lord Byron! (4)
7. I cart corn about the estate in which Herriot-Watt Univ. stands! (9)
8. Knighted Scottish author, poet, and critic who married Charlotte Carpentier in 1797 (3, 6, 5)
13. Loving tins manufactured in West Lothian industrial centre? (10)
15. Scottish king who, with number, becomes 1012 victor over the Danes at Cruden Bay! (7, 2)
17. Pelts? Tat, having been skinned most evenly! (8)
20. Motoring organization about to have tea in the middle of Stewart House in Duror, Argyllshire! (6)
23. Arose, changed and sailed to uninhabited island near Mull! (5)
24. Clan I like to see partly daubed with indigo! (4)

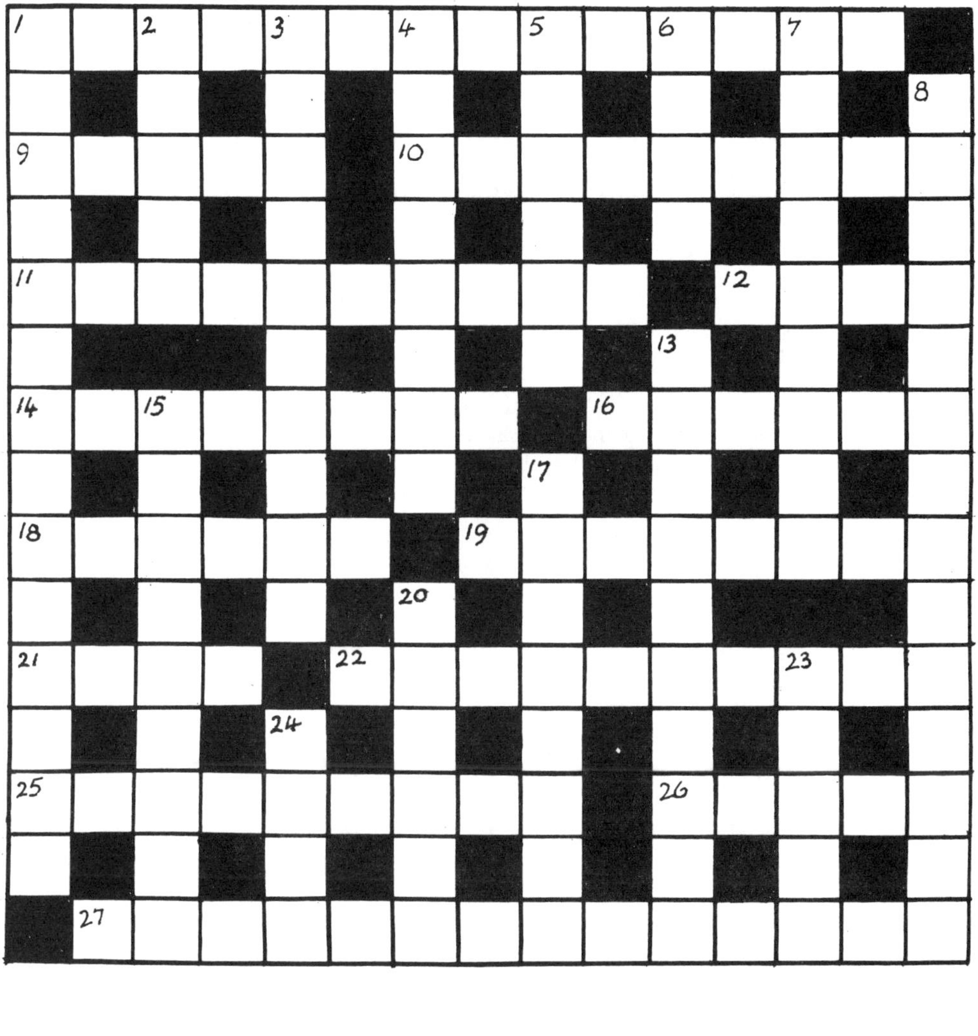
1
2
3
4
5
6
7
8
9
10
11
12
13
14
15
16
17
18
19
20
21
22
23
24
25
26
27

58

ACROSS

1. Where the Scenic Route comes to an end? (4, 2, 8)
9. Inverness-shire water which upset client with chore? (4, 6)
10. Secret part of a tavern used for standing weapons on end? (4)
12. Ancient ruined castle of the Gordons near Fyvie, Aberdeenshire where the beheaded might get a new leading force? (5)
13. That part of a wabster's loom where he keeps his beer, perhaps? (6)
16. Commonwealth bowling champion made of the same stuff as his bowls? (4)
17. Surname of one of Mary, Queen of Scots, famous "Four Maries" who married John, 2nd son of Lord Semphill. (10)
19. I dig up Perth countryside, it's the very place for the family of Fingask! (10)
20. Make case out for the ancient Gaelic letter equating to an 'a' as in 'cat'! (4)
22. Spread a ranch with an old plaid worn by Scotsmen? (6)
23. The 'wee' magistrate whose memory is preserved on the tall Celtic Cross seen before entering Kirkmichael in Perthshire! (5)
26. A single Scot living in Torranyard? (4)
27. Upland area near Alness in Easter Ross – H.L.I. rules it! (5, 4)
28. Volcanic group of uninhabited islands lying off the coast of Mull, noted for their seal communities (9, 5)

DOWN

2. Tibetan beast, we hear, can be source of great perplexity to the Scots! (4)
3. A little hesitation fusing with start of capital in huge forest near Loch Awe, Argyllshire? (6)
4. I chaff idle gossip about ancient ruined fortress near Mintlaw, Aberdeenshire! (10)
5. Anything Scottish – a mixture of hot and cold start! (4)
6. Lantern hit about Angus area – ancient home of the Ogilvy family? (10)
7. Scottish breed good for selling toffee, perhaps? (8, 6)
8. Indian tribe with liquid centre camped on Arran? (14)
11. Ayrshire town which was designated a 'Baronial Burgh' by James VI in 1585 and which in 1876, changed its status to 'Police Burgh' (5)
14. Chore racer has to perform in Aberdeenshire estate, west of Tarland? (10)
15. Being rampant, Scot should not stick his proverbial head here! (5, 5)
18. Perth whisky-making family warned about losing number! (5)
21. Easter Ross village full of winding lanes leading to street-head? (6)
24. Make a case for Tarbet, Uist? (4)
25. Old Scots comedian will come from here, by the sounds of it! (4)

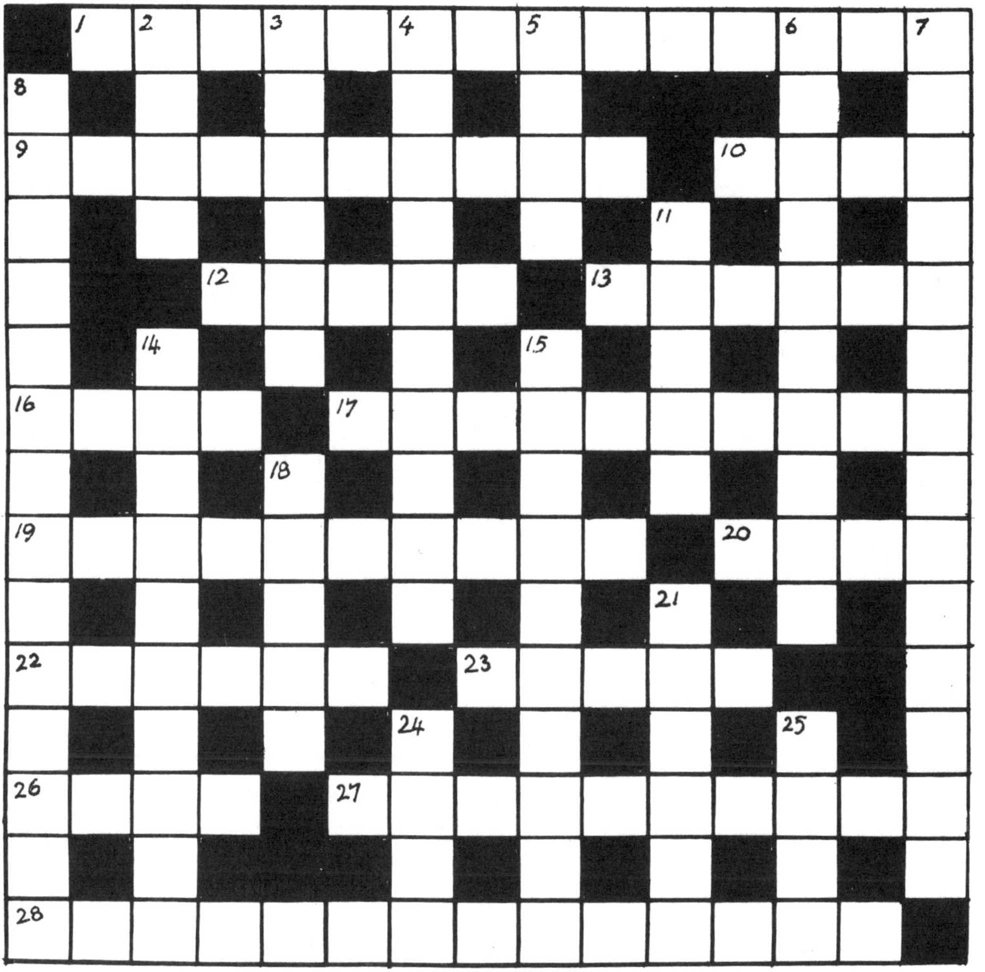
1
2
3
4
5
6
7
8
9
10
11
12
13
14
15
16
17
18
19
20
21
22
23
24
25
26
27
28

59

ACROSS

1. Toil about after sweet cake, tasty village sitting above Loch Ness in the Great Glen! (7)
5. Acts upon Scottish lands? (7)
9. Aberdeen associate in the cattle business? (5)
10. Village east of Inverness re.'Dear Sir'? (9)
11. Ponder a Hebridean island? (4)
12. Scotland's capital seized a small horn? (5)
13. "How can ye chant ye little birds, — — sae weary, fu' o' care" (Burns: The Banks o' Doon) (3,1)
16. "— Garbh Airde". A headland on Seil Island, Argyllshire, popular with tourists because of its remarkable frog-like shape (5)
18. Stretch of water — a good place to dunk baby's biscuit in Perthshire? (5,4)
20. Highland river to speak on large Morayshire district? (9)
23. The German always becomes the Scots great northern diver! (5)
25. "While we sit bousing at the nappy, An' getting fou' and — happy" (Burns: Tam O' Shanter) (4)
26. Mary has upset a thousand with old Scots kitchen spoon!(5)
27. Lady coming to a point while ski-ing in large Perthshire glen? (4)
31. Title of one of the informative books written by 2 down in his series "The Queen's Scotland" (9)
32. Border village in which a herb comes to nothing? (5)
33. Sad, rein in confusion in Scots cavalryman's left-hand area? (7)
34. Modern stag with large Aberdeenshire village as his territory? (3,4)

DOWN

1. Em, Barra seen as gathering place? (7)

2,4. Contemporary Scottish author of historical and geographical books on his native land (see 31 across) (5,7)

3. In former times, the Scottish name for the fibrous stuff put in inkwells to prevent spilling (4)
4. See 2.
5. Ascot Gold Cup winner coming from hamlet in Easter Ross? (7)
6. Argyllshire village centre of American car industry? (4)
7. Misty morn encircling craig on Grampian peak? (9)
8. Sikh, 'ger plies with whisky? (7)
14. Skim over a line of glacial hills flanking the River Don in Aberdeenshire? (5)
15. Auchtermuchty rievers seen in civil parish in the Buchan area of Aberdeen? (5)
17. Break with early arrival at prehistoric dwelling site in Argyllshire? (9)
19. Moultrie Kelsall's part played last month? (3)
20. Hues can be seen to good effect in scattered Aberdeenshire village! (7)
21. Laud age of the ancient MacNeal lairdship on the east coast of Kintyre? (7)
22. Radio man's room? — just the place to see international football by the sound of it! (7)
24. Rome air turbulent having been the site of the Battle of Corrichie in 1562! (7)
28. A circular oval, or horse-shoe shaped structure of stones surrounded by a bank or ditch. Scotland's supreme example is Urquhart Churchyard on the shores of the Cromarty Firth (5)
29. Claret Uist keeps in a small case? (4)
30. Mo? She's to be found in the direction of Stranraer with a smile on her face! (4)

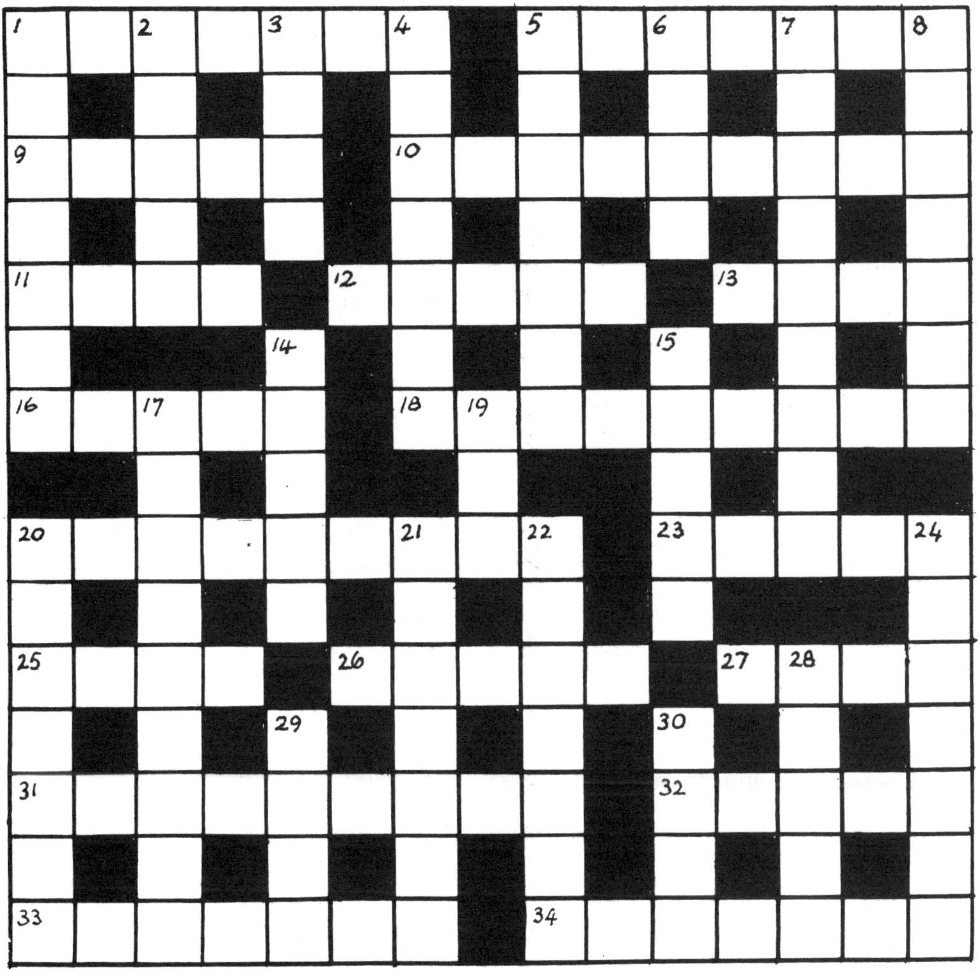

60

ACROSS

1. Aberdeen – the 'Mecca' for hard rock enthusiasts? (7, 4)
9. STV political presenter De Burgh has to embrace a duck! (4)
10. Huish ace? all found it upsetting in Glasgow street! (11)
11. Turns up at Dundee's park with the shaft of a scythe! (4)
14. English poet at Dunnet Head – soiled with soot! (7)
17. Peat piler is a sorry man, we hear! (5)
18. "I'm truly sorry man's dominion, Has broken nature's social ——" (Burns: To a Mouse) (5)
19. See 14 down.
20. A narrow strip of wood covering a hundred with a slate! (5)
21. I list, break down and have fallen behind! (5)
22. Former Easter Ross fishing village in which to rein in five? (5)
23. Reaches right after Skye upset? (5)
24. Silver recently found in former noble Galloway family? (5)
25. Scots wife with hot hundred dancing – shake with laughter! (7)
29. Urquhart initially backward but then becomes gushing! (4)
32. Scots river valley with Wells' first becomes famous Perthshire school! (11)
33. Wag returning – a constant reminder he's a fool! (4)
34. Former home of Scots philanthropist Andrew Carnegie (5, 6)

DOWN

2. Tatum's dad seen near Stranraer? (4)
3. Auld combines with him – the devil! (4)
4. Hard tackler included in Menstrie Rangers squad? (5)
5. Chartered accountant at Hootenanny beginning with cry at 'hide-and-seek'! (5)
6. I let you first cut up a slice! (5)
7. Fired Lewis, for example – sent to east coast shipbuilding centre! (11)
8. Gin-makers place? good for educating royality in Scotland! (11) . . .
12. . . . and Sir Hugh has his place nearby! (11)
13. Glasgow area for fish and chips beginnings we hear! (11)

14, 19 across. Former Scottish bank for U.K. textile workers, perhaps? (7, 5)

15. A water-baliff would make a stern headmaster by the sound of it! (5)
16. Tricked, we hear, Scots comedian Laurel in Border village? (7)
19. Scottish title from a lot about five? (5)
26. Scots' bustle within upon taking office? (5)
27. Ascended hill with a hundred little sheep? (5)
28. The moral of Elizabeth I, cutting off Mary's head? (5)

30, 31. Goal slam seen up Angus peak! (4, 4)

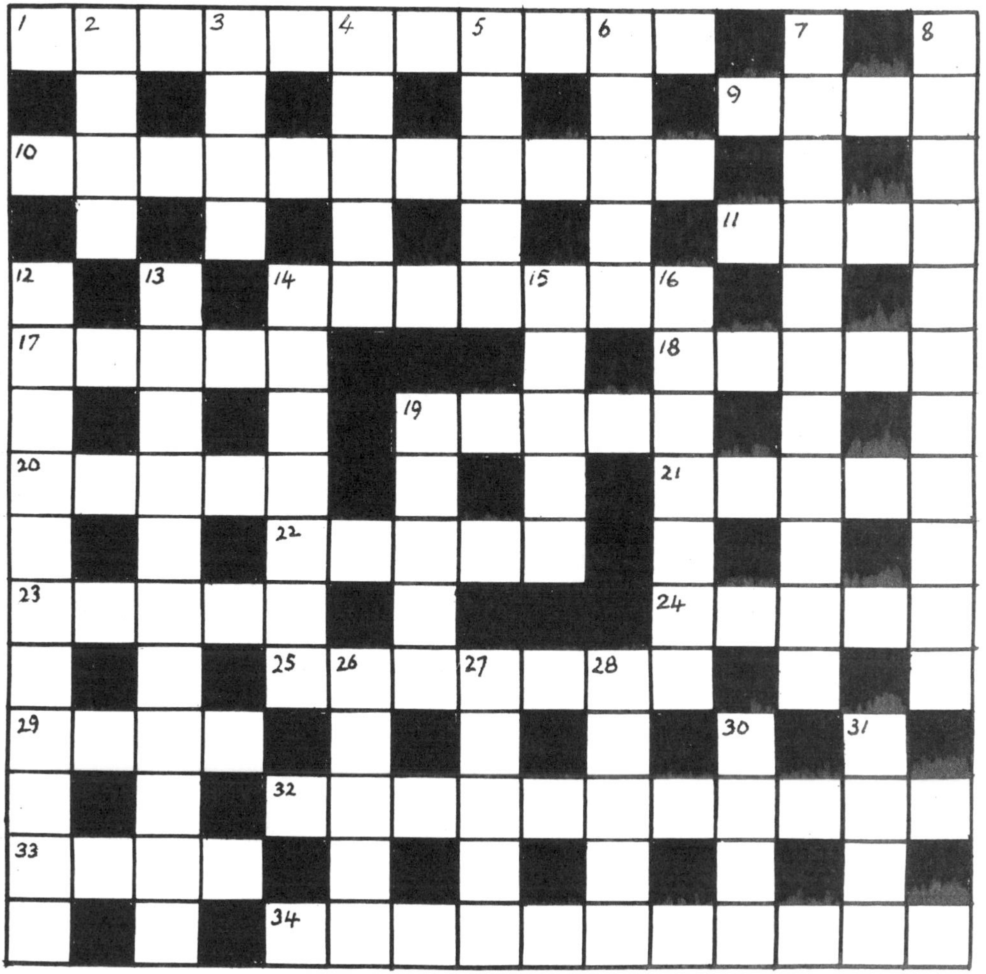

Solutions

1

ACROSS: 1. Cromarty, 5. Tarmac, 9. Rowallan, 10. Quinie, 12. Oolats, 13. Cardross, 15. Ardnamurchan, 18. Presbyterian, 23. Talisker, 24. See 28., 26. Agyaun, 27. Braeside, 28. Silver Tassie, 29. Clarinda.

DOWN: 1. Carson, 2. Orwell, 3. Ally-tor, 4. Teal, 6. Anunder, 7. Munlochy, 8. Cressing, 11. Panmure, 14. Snitter, 16. Spittals, 17. Ben Loyal, 19. Bascule, 20. Amateur, 21. Ossian, 22. Geneva, 25. Bril.

2

ACROSS: 1. Gareloch, 5. Spiter, 9. Aviemore, 10. Outram, 11. Sheraton, 12. Adamic, 14. Isle of Yell, 18. Moray Firth, 22. Lyness, 23. Kill-door, 24. Eldrin, 25. St. Mirren, 26. Tummel, 27. Anderson.

DOWN: 1. Ghaist, 2. Raivel, 3. Lymfad, 4. Carnoustie, 6. Plum-duff, 7. Thrammel, 8. R.S. McColl, 13. West Linton, 15. Smollett, 16. Ardnadam, 17. Ayrshire, 19. Blaise, 20. Forres, 21. Crinan.

3

ACROSS: 1. Wishart, 5. Cast-ewe, 9. Sever, 10. Newbattle, 11. Ransevall, 12. Arran, 13. Yield, 15. Lochnagar, 18. Antoninus, 19. Nevil, 21. Ratho, 23. Oliphants, 25. Rampar-eel, 26. Laive, 27. Eard-din, 28. Stewles.

DOWN: 1. Westray, 2. St. Vincent, 3. Airie, 4. Tantallon, 5. Cowal, 6. Slamannan, 7. Etter, 8. Eleanor, 14. Dundonald, 16. Cassillis, 17. Govanhill, 18. Airdrie, 20. Lissens, 22. Tamer, 23. Odeon, 24. Halse.

4

ACROSS: 1. Asil, 4. Plough, 9. Mull of Galloway, 11. Loch Broom, 12. Roman, 13. Manage, 15. Clairach, 17. Loch Earn, 18. Shaird, 21. Nodal, 22. Maclellan, 24. Silver Darlings, 25. Snotty, 26. Fyne.

DOWN: 2. Scowb, 3. Lugton, 4. Pell-mell, 5. O poortith, 6. Graemsay Island, 7. Emblem, 8. Clach-na-Cudainn, 10. Inch, 14. Glenlivet, 16. Cromarty, 17. Long, 19. Danish, 20. Sclaff, 23. Ellon.

5

ACROSS: 1. Firth of Clyde, 9. Pivotally, 10. Udall, 11. Runcie, 12. Wedgwood, 13. Maiden, 14. Fair Isle, 17. Hamilton, 19. Crieff, 21. Misseems, 23. Sneeze, 25. Clort, 26. Dundonald, 27. Burke and Hare.

DOWN: 2. Irvingism, 3. Titline, 4. Ooly, 5. Clyde Law, 6. Younger, 7. Erato, 8. Flodden Field, 9. Portmahomack, 15. Skewed air, 16. Polmadie, 18. Leester, 20. Rannoch, 22. Scowb, 24. Anan.

6

ACROSS: 1. Minto House, 6. Ness, 10. Cowal, 11. Duntocher, 12. See 7., 13. Hiant, 15. Nat Muir, 17. Schemes, 19. Unequal, 21. Coracle, 22. Nyapp, 24. Cranston, 27. River Leet, 28. Niall, 29. Horn, 30. Keir Hardie.

DOWN: 1. Muck, 2. Newbattle, 3. Oil Up, 4. Old Deer, 5. Singles, 7. Ethna Campbell, 8. Strathspey, 9. Loch Mhor, 14. Angus North, 16. Usurpers, 18. MacDonald, 20. Loch Ewe, 21. Chanter, 23. Aiver, 25. Sanna, 26. Blae.

7

ACROSS: 1. Henry Bell, 8. Unapool, 9. Rigouts, 10. Abertay, 13. I lang hae, 14. Ream, 16. Tulliallan, 20. Gosk, 22. Gyre, 24. Cristendie, 28. Asta, 29. Waajerer, 31. Barnage, 34. Tamteen, 35. Raeburn, 36. Thrustles.

DOWN: 2. Nag-nail, 3. Young, 4. Eeswall, 5. Luna, 6. Spur, 7. Clayock, 12 & 25. Tam O'Shanter, 15. Agin, 17. Ury, 18. Lees, 19. Ascaig, 21. Ski, 22 & 11. Gilbert Burnet, 23. Rair, 26. Dornell, 27. Errands, 30 & 1. down. James Herriot, 32. Nebb, 33. Eent

8

ACROSS: 3. Midlothian, 8. Affric, 9. S.T.U.C., 10. Kilmarnock, 11. Hob, 13, 25 down. Lion Rampant, 14. Aberlour, 16. Nane, 18. Alban, 21. Minch, 23. Marr, 26. Malvinas, 27. Nith, 28. Caa, 29. Jean Peters, 30. Thou, 31. Nicoll, 32. Parliament

DOWN: 1, 27 down. Official Notice, 2. Drymen, 3. McGrain, 4. Donovan, 5. Omsk, 6. Inchmoan, 7. Newburgh, 12. Drum, 15. Bear, 17. Alma, 18. Army Camp, 19. Ballater, 20. Neil, 22. Cottrell, 24. Astarte, 25. see 13 across, 27. see 1 down, 29. Jura

9

ACROSS: 1. Suddart, 5. Stacher, 9. Ross and Cromarty, 10. Target, 12. Elliot, 13. Eisen, 15. Nick on, 16. Darger, 17. Nar fu', 18. Mackie, 19. Rennie, 21. Noble, 22. Stuart, 24. Scaups, 28. Lochleven Castle, 29. Muldoon, 30. Halcyon.

DOWN: 1. Stretan. 2. District Council, 3. Agate, 4. Tade, 5. Sorn, 6. Ammel, 7. Herring Industry, 8. Royster, 11. Tennent, 12. Endures, 14. Scrub, 18. Mashlam, 20. Eastern, 23. Rollo, 25. Crail, 26. Avon, 27. Inch.

10

ACROSS: 1. Rothesay, 5. Smelts, 9. Bathgate, 10. Plener, 12. Roopit, 13. Rowallan, 15. Whittinghame, 18. Innerleithen, 23. Crawford, 24. Usurer. 26. Pattle, 27. Colonsay, 28. Earest, 29. Montrose.

DOWN: 1. Robert, 2. Tattoo, 3. English, 4. Aits, 6. Mallaig, 7. Langle At, 8. Stranger, 11. Popists, 14. At Heart, 16. Pitcaple, 17. Ancaster, 19. Ruffles, 20. Eishort, 21. Presto, 22. Argyle, 25. Polo.

11

ACROSS: 1. Bonnie Prince Charlie, 9. Water-Corn, 10. Cock o', 11. Inring, 12. Morrison, 13. Lauder, 14. The Minch, 17. Gangsman, 19. McEwan, 21. Gateside, 23. Gavall, 25. Maain, 26. Linklater, 27. Kinlochleven.

DOWN: 2. Otterburn, 3. Nirange, 4. Enow, 5. Rannochy, 6. Nechram, 7. Eecks, 8. Corn-Chandler, 9. Whirlygigums, 15. Newbattle, 16. Gardyloo, 18. Sussnin, 20. See 1 across., 22. Traik, 24. Inch.

12

ACROSS: 1. See 17, 6. Scad, 10. Routing, 11. Unicorn, 12. McAlister, 13. Hynde, 14. China, 15. The Triple Crown, 17. Rank is but the guineas stamp, 20. Yates, 21. Orson, 23. Lord Arran, 25. Abaiser, 26. Endless, 27. Dips, 28. Coatbridge.

DOWN: 1. Thrum, 2. Education, 3. Utilitarianism, 4. Night at, 5. Amulree, 7. See 15 across, 8. Danderers, 9. Sir Harry Lauder, 14. Cardonald, 16. Peterhead, 18. Balerno, 19. Tarbert, 22. See 17, 24. Nosie.

13

ACROSS: 1. Jock Stein, 6. Lewis, 9. Tryst, 10. Lord Brown, 11. Stevenston, 12. Spey, 14. Quillon, 15. Kennedy, 17. Eleanor, 19. Squeeze, 20. Nent, 22. Hyter-styte, 25. Newcastle, 26. Utole, 27. Every, 28. Northbyes.

DOWN: 1. Jutes, 2. Clydeside, 3. Sutherland, 4. Ellison, 5. Norfolk, 6. Libo, 7. Whoop, 8. Sandy Lyle, 13. Angus South, 14. Queen Anne, 16. Everybody, 18. Royston, 19. Sye-beer, 21. Nowte, 23. Evens, 24. Mary.

14

ACROSS: 1. Airdrie, 5. Lendrum, 9. Kenny Dalglish, 10. Riccarton, 11. Nuncio, 12. See 9, 14. Ontak, 15. Lyke-waker, 18. Macintyre, 20. Nowed, 22. Lockhart, 24. Weebis, 26. Gasoliery, 27. Tatti, 28. Raeloch, 29. Skearie.

DOWN: 1. Arkinholm, 2. Run-knot, 3. Roy Aitken, 4. Earn, 5. Loch Arklet, 6. Nyarg, 7. Rottick, 8. Minch, 13. Allycriesh, 16. Wanrestie, 17. Redeswire, 19. Cocks e'e, 21. Wabster, 22. Lugar, 23. Hell o', 25. Dybs.

15

ACROSS: 1. Cashell, 5. Provost, 9. Innes, 10. Scrabster, 11. Napier, 12. Whithorn, 14. Oread, 15. Ochiltree, 18. Macgregor, 20. Creed, 22. Armament, 24. Fraser, 26. Stranraer, 27. Neill, 28. Rannoch, 29. Trapeze.

DOWN: 1. Cairngorm, 2. Sand-pie, 3. Eastender, 4. Luss, 5. Perthshire, 6. Oobit, 7. Outgoer, 8. Thren, 13. Lough Neagh, 16. Lochranza, 17. Elderslie, 19. Cameron, 21. Erskine, 22. Arser, 23. Munro, 25. Wrat.

16

ACROSS: 1. Magdalene, 6. Stram, 9. Relic, 10. Grammatic, 11. Real Estate, 12. Rona, 14. Ephebus, 15. Newkirk, 17. Bernard Gallacher, 19. The Ruin, 20. Tain, 22. Donaghadee, 25. Lamberton, 26. Afton, 27. Darer, 28. Mary Tudor.

DOWN: 1. Morar, 2. See 17, 3. Auchenblae 4. Ergates, 5. Evanton, 6. Syme, 7. Ratho, 8. McCracken, 13. Sweetheart, 14. Embattled, 16. Inundated, 18. Drostam, 19. Trainer, 21. Immer, 23. Enner, 24. Deer.

17

ACROSS: 1. See 11, 4. Scribe, 8. Weir of Hermiston, 10. Robertson, 11. Allan Evans, 12. Yarrow, 14. Scritors, 16. McHattie, 17. Snifle, 20. Beano, 21. Elderslie, 23. Nationalisation, 24. Tether, 25. Ethik.

DOWN: 1. Edinburgh Castle, 2. Atour, 3. Schist, 4. Screnoch, 5. Ruination, 6. Battle of Falkirk, 7. Owerby, 9. Nanes, 13. Ostrogoth, 15. River Ayr, 16. Mabon, 18. Exeunt, 19. Advise, 22. Reath.

18

ACROSS: 1. Linlithgow, 6. See 14 across, 10. Guttler, 11. Knabsie, 12. Lassockie, 13. Maria, 14. Scapa Flow, 15. Eastriggs, 17. Glengarry, 20. Leese, 21. Ringe, 23. Barlanark, 25. Loch Ewe, 26. Intrals, 27. Yell, 28. Stagherers.

DOWN: 1. Legal, 2. Nithsdale, 3. Isle of Anglesey, 4. Harikle, 5. Orkneys, 7. Leser, 8. Wae wags ye (!), 9. Balmoral Castle, 14. Sugar-ally, 16. Glenadale, 18. Rebleat, 19. Yarking, 22. Nicol, 24. Kists.

19

ACROSS: 1. Black-bitch, 9. Hall, 10. Sniftering, 11. Gemm ba', 12. Balerno, 15. Steerer, 16. Gusts, 17. Gack, 18. Lulu, 19. Recur, 21. Palaver, 22. Monarch, 24. Voggie, 27. Drumlanrig, 28. Nyat, 29. Sunset Song.

DOWN: 2. Lang, 3. Coffee, 4. Beeling, 5. Tain, 6. Hoggets, 7. Lammermuir, 8. Clear Rough, 12. Bog-spavins, 13. Loch Laggan, 14. Outer, 15. Strum, 19. Remedes, 20. Rocklie, 23. Amands, 25. Gunn, 26. Pirn.

20

ACROSS: 1. Rittocks, 5. Banjie, 9. Ayrshire, 10. Finart, 11. Laverock, 12. Knible, 14. Inverclyde, 18. Eightpence, 22. See 13 down, 23. Egyptian, 24. Sogers, 25. Roberton, 26. Nisser, 27. Seceders.

DOWN: 1. Read'ly, 2. Thrave, 3. Others, 4. Kirkconnel, 6. Alien Act, 7. Jean Boyd, 8. Eitheren, 13. & 22. Beechgrove Garden, 15. Ferguson, 16. Aggreges, 17. St. George, 19. Speere, 20. Kiltie, 21. Snangs.

21

ACROSS: 3. Glenrothes, 8. Ackrer, 9. Item, 10. James Scott, 11. Mel, 13. Abee, 14. See 24, 15. Cole, 17, 3 down & 30 across. Lewis Grassic Gibbon, 20. Linge, 22. Leer, 24. Wembley Wizards, 25. Cree, 27. Ean, 28. Blairessan, 29. Eese, 30. See 17, 31. Easter Ross.

DOWN: 1. Scrabble, 2. Grieve, 3. See 17, 4. Ellon, 5. Rait, 6. Hammerin', 7. Seil Isle, 12. Izel, 14. Wede, 16. Oily, 17. Lawrence, 18. Waminess, 19. Sole, 21. Glenavon, 23. Run-rigs, 25. Cast by, 26. Ratho, 28. Bear.

22

ACROSS: 1. Romager, 5. Twal-cup, 9. See 29, 10. The Crags o' Tumbledown Mountain, 11. Attact, 12. See 10, 14. Inner, 15. Utteridge, 18. September, 20. Naper, 22. Wark-leem, 24. Tenors, 26. Brie-stone, 27. India, 28. St. Eunan, 29. Kinneil Kerse.

DOWN: 1. Rik-ma-tiks, 2. Maryton, 3. Glencarse, 4. Reth, 5. The Cotters, 6. Arran, 7. Cog-hand, 8. Pooin, 13. See 10, 16. Rankenian, 17. Earlshall, 19. Perfite, 21. Proadge, 22. Webis, 23. Losin, 25. Yerk.

23

ACROSS: 1. Cross Cairn, 6. Pert, 10. Scharge, 11. Irisher, 12. Enlarging, 13. See 3, 14. Garth, 15. Estalment, 17. Brearding, 20. Other, 21. Ratho, 23. Glen Clova, 25. St. Blane, 26. Loolorn, 27. Eith, 28. Wapinschaw.

DOWN: 1. Cosie, 2. Ochiltree, 3. & 13. across Sir Arthur Conan Doyle, 4. Averile, 5. Raingit, 7. Echay, 8. Tormentor, 9. Kildalton Cross, 14. Gaberosie, 16. Ech-Nor-Och, 18. Ingle-wa, 19. Glen Lui, 22. Tabet, 24. Agnew.

24

ACROSS: 1 & 9. Campbells Are Coming, 6. Gorse, 10. Shand, 12. Snosh, 13. Merry-mass, 14. Spean, 16. Smatterie, 19. Braeriach, 20. Pinge, 21. Scots-room, 23. Egger, 26. Tirry, 27. Cairngorm, 28. Claff, 29. Advertish.

DOWN: 2. Arran, 3. Pech-stane, 4. Eams, 5. Linsey MacDonald, 7. Ogham, 8. Sandsting, 11. Grute, 15. Parochial, 17. Edingight, 18. Kirry, 22. Tarff, 24. Earms, 25. Urie

25

ACROSS: 1. Arbuthnott, 6. Baub, 10. Blair, 11. Ian McColl, 12. Skreaghs, 13. Ranza, 15. Glasgow, 17. Larbert, 19 & 24. Eilean A Chalmain, 21. Bow-Haun, 22. Blaff, 27. Ochilview, 28. Usher, 29. Neep, 30. Fecklessly

DOWN: 1. Alba, 2. Blackhall, 3. Tiree, 4. Neil Gow, 5. Tinesel, 7. Aboon, 8. Ballantyne, 9. Scarcraw, 14. Agnes Broun, 16. Goat Fell, 18. Evanishes, 20. Ascrive, 21. Blakwak, 23. Ashie, 25. Maule, 26. Croy.

26

ACROSS: 1. Alloa Athletic, 8. MacBeth, 9. Niddrie, 11. Averon, 13. Screeger, 15. Lulls, 16. Leswalt, 18. Balevil, 19. Barra, 21. Dallachs, 23. Sydera, 25. Exament, 26. Melrose Abbey, 28. Broughty Ferry

DOWN: 2. Locheil, 3. Ore, 4. Ache, 5. Hynd Castle, 6. Eadie, 7. Irrogat, 8. Meall Buidhe, 10. Earl's Palace. 12. Ousel, 14. Clove hitch, 17. See 26., 18. Balgair, 20. Raemoir, 22. Aye-fu', 24. Amry, 27. Lye

27

ACROSS: 1. Onlife, 4. Osenbrug, 9. Bugars, 10. Drambuie, 12. Into, 13. Stott, 14. Gleg, 17. Hamilton Park, 20. Earl of Wemyss, 23. Ring of Bright, 24. Javel, 25. Deny, 28. Galloway, 29. Grieve, 30. E'estanes, 31. Barnes.

DOWN: 1. See 23., 2. Legitims, 3. Fire, 5. Strathpeffer, 6. Nimp, 7. Raucle, 8. Gledge, 11. Atholl Palace, 15. Sleat, 16. Treen, 18. Syneteen, 19. Assypets, 21. Tragle, 22. Inglis, 26. Iona, 27. Orra.

28

ACROSS: 1. Punchik, 5. Waddell, 9. Rowan, 10. Labouring, 11. St. Andrews, 12. Essie, 13. Yates, 15. Royal Scot, 18. Pleasance, 19. Nauks, 21. Oakie, 23. Suppie-mae, 25. Carradale, 26. Licht, 27. Yeather, 28. Neypsie.

DOWN: 1. Portsoy, 2. Newbattle, 3. Haned, 4. Kilkerran, 5. Webis, 6. Drumellan, 7. Exies, 8. Laggert, 14. Sassenach, 16. Yeelpreen, 17. Crummocks, 18. Proochy, 20. Sheltie, 22. Korka, 23. Stair, 24. Islay.

29

ACROSS: 3. Ballantrae, 8 & 9. Safari Park, 10. See 26., 11. Eel, 13. Lour, 14. Landart, 15. Swee, 17. Eiden, 20. Mason, 22. Ream, 24. Selkirk, 25. Odds, 27. W.R.I., 28. Calton Hill, 29. Alva, 30. See 26., 31. Dearth-caps.

DOWN: 1. See 14., 2. Cawdor, 3. Birness, 4. Ladle, 5. Awps, 6. Rokelays, 7. Embleton 12. Snam, 14. Lena Zavaroni, 16. Wark, 17. Eastwood, 18. Dalriada, 19. Neil, 21. Old Clune, 23. McColls, 25. Oghams, 26. Flora MacDonald's Lament, 28. Cath.

30

ACROSS: 1. Byrness, 5. Dreeful, 9. Total, 10. Dunimarle, 11. Onless, 12. Catsherd, 14. Nanna, 15. Dogfoolie, 18. Caledonia, 20. Ethie, 22. Cumbered, 24. Isings, 26. Elderslie, 27. Afore, 28. Kintyre, 29. Laggert.

DOWN: 1. Bethoc-Nic, 2. Rathlin, 3. Ellisland, 4. Sade, 5. Duncan Gray, 6. Emmis, 7. Fordell, 8. Leend, 13. Edinbellie, 16. Overscaig, 17. Enelsheet, 19. Lumsden, 21. Henhole, 22. Check, 23. Early, 25. Yell.

31

ACROSS: 1. Stirling Castle, 5. See 1 across, 9. Inveresk, 10. See 34.,12. Rink-medal, 14. Alloo, 15. Ann, 16. Scried, 19. Dreet, 22. Recur, 23. Gnarry, 25. Bur, 28. Tutor, 29. Allermuir, 32. Elands, 33. Agricola, 34. Sydney Devine, 35. Needment.

DOWN: 1. Shirra, 2. Irvine, 3. Larum, 4. Nosed, 6. & 20. Alexander Brothers, 7. Taillyer, 8. Eyemouth, 11. Pladda, 13. Ear, 17. Corbridge, 18. Ingram, 20. See 6., 21. Scotland, 24. Rae, 26. Fusome, 27. Creast, 30. Logie, 31. Rhind.

32

ACROSS: 1. Bonnybridge, 9. Staw, 10. Kelvingrove, 11. Lake, 14. Breells, 17. Idill, 18. Ethik, 19. Barry, 20. Nairn, 21. Arnot, 22. Tunes, 23. Aigre, 24. Errol, 25. Rafford, 29. Pate, 32. Cock-a-leekie, 33. Nine, 34. Celtic Cross.

DOWN: 2. Ox-e'e, 3. Nave, 4. Bonar, 5. Ier-oe, 6. Gavel, 7. Strathendry, 8. Tweed Kettle, 12. Lion Rampant, 13. Livingstone, 14. Blenter, 15. Largs, 16. Seyaled, 19. Banff, 26. Avoke, 27. Fiket, 28. Relic, 30. Deer, 31. Liss.

33

ACROSS: 1. Shetland, 5. Millan, 9. Lochmore, 10. Evened, 11. Spirital, 12. Cromie, 14. Ashiestiel, 18. Loch Slapin, 22. Natrie, 23. Eglinton, 24. Yammer, 25. St. Manire, 26. Ernist, 27. Inverewe.

DOWN: 1. Splash, 2. Eechie, 3. Lammie, 4. Norman's Law, 6. Inveresk, 7. Longmuir, 8. Nidgells, 13. Livingston, 15. Blantyre, 16. Scotsman, 17. Assizers, 19. Dilate, 20. Strive, 21. Sneeze.

34

ACROSS: 7. Out-town Multure, 9. Storgs, 10. Discerne, 11. Arbirlot, 13. Achtoo, 14. Pang, 15. Clout, 16. Mamp, 17. Thysel, 19. Skellums, 21. Cochbell, 23. Report, 24. O saw ye my dearie.

DOWN: 1. Contermashious, 2. Stirling, 3. Doosil, 4. Kned, 5. Dunshalt, 6. Streah, 8. Random Memories, 12. Tross, 15. Colleges, 16. Millport, 18. Schowy, 20. Earmer, 22. Layt.

35

ACROSS: 1. Sutherland, 6. Sned, 10. Cearc, 11. Newington, 12. Nicolson, 13. Elder, 15. Egilsay, 17. Evanton, 19. Schafts, 21. America, 22. Ethie, 24. Kirkwall, 27. Kenneller, 28. Duart, 29. Tuam, 30. Inverallan.

DOWN: 1. Seck, 2. Teaninich, 3. Elcho, 4. Lindsay, 5. Newance, 7. Noted, 8. Dundrennan, 9. Inverawe, 14. Wee, sleekit, 16. Sufferer, 18. Thirlwall, 20. Sikklen, 21. Airdrie, 23. Handa, 25. Wad na', 26. Sten.

36

ACROSS: 1. Gospel Lad, 6. Tacht, 9. Ill-e' e 10. Naitir-woo, 11. Huferie, 12. Knurlin, 14. Alexandria, 15. Isla, 18. Aith, 19. Commanding, 23. Hen-sure, 25. Scoured, 26. Blackhill, 27. Upgae, 28. Tylie, 29. Green-belt.

DOWN: 1. See 17., 2. Sclaffert, 3. Even-Road, 4. Lang e'ed, 5. Drink wi', 6. Trig up, 7. Cowal, 8. Two, 13. Near-geddert, 16. Shirragle, 17. An Comunn Gaidhealach, 20. Overing, 21. Mashlie, 22. Ruskie, 24. Niall, 26. Bat.

37

ACROSS: 1. Milngavie, 8, 9 & 14. Sir Alec Douglas-Home, 10. Saddell, 13. Unilever, 14. See 8., 16. Eigg Island, 20. Oner, 22. Reem, 24. John Walker, 28. Smoo, 29. Swanston, 31. Present, 34. Rankine, 35. Cathkin, 36. Athenaeum.

DOWN: 1. Mid-Bute, 2. Louping, 3. Gylie, 4. Veshell, 5. Esks, 6. Maid, 7. Scalder, 11. Ashdow, 12. Eden, 15. Moil, 17. Ime, 18. Gemm, 19. St. John, 21. Eme, 22. Reppoch, 23. Esse, 25. Naworth, 26. Katrine, 27. Rin-Seam, 30. Ninon, 32. Sohs, 33. Tina.

38

ACROSS: 1. Birnam, 5. Biggar, 8. Crail, 9. Orwell, 10. Aitken, 11. Erper, 14. Hundalee, 16. Stanse, 18. Haddingtonshire, 20. Ben Lui, 22. Whitrope, 25. Galop, 27. Dortor, 28. Almond, 29. Aucht, 30. Nickum, 31. Haydon.

DOWN: 1. Brooch, 2. Rawn, 3. McLellan, 4. Campbeltown Loch, 5. Blarts, 6. Gike, 7. Runcie, 12. A-Diddle, 13. Lathers, 15. Udale, 17. Strip, 19. Neidpath, 20. Bowden, 21. Ingram, 23. Elsdon, 24. Eric, 26. Ford.

39

ACROSS: 1. Bathgate, 5. Knarks, 9. Neppiter, 10. Twizel, 12. Innes, 13. Elizabeth, 14. Nationalist, 18. Draigle-tail, 21. Lou Macari, 22. Barst, 23. Turchy, 24. Legitime, 25. Ackers, 26. Ase-holes.

DOWN: 1. Ben Hiant, 2. Tap-o'-Noth, 3. Gliss, 4. There was a lad, 6. Newbattle, 7. Rizzer, 8. Selcht, 11. Aikie Guineas, 15. Old Machar, 16. Barrhill, 17. Blethers, 19. Flotta, 20. Hurrok, 22. Beith.

40

ACROSS: 1. Billy Connolly, 10. Freedom, 11. Ancroft, 12 & 13. Alan Breck, 14. Hogg, 17. Middlin, 18. Tweedle, 19. New Mill, 22. Rossini, 24 & 16. Wild Geese, 25. Stabs, 26. Trig, 29. Evading, 30. Looten o', 31. Redeswire Raid.

DOWN: 2. Ireland, 3. Lady, 4. Cameron, 5. Near-cut, 6. Oich, 7. Leopold, 8. A fragment when, 9. Staggering Bob, 15. Blair, 16. See 24., 20. Wallace, 21. Lithgow, 22. Rabbler, 23. Israeli, 27. Fife, 28. Poor.

41

ACROSS: 1. Robb, 3. Again-call, 9. Tilt. 10. Calderpark, 12. Loch Ness, 13. Methil, 14. Bakehouse Close, 18. Magdalen Chapel, 20. Uncoly, 22. Bengiels, 24. Glen Creran, 25. Sybo, 26. Gray Geese, 27. Tean.

DOWN: 1. Ruttle, 2. Bill Craig, 4. Gladstone, 5. Inds. 6. Corn Exchange, 7. Leath, 8. Skillet, 11. Inverallochy, 15. Secretars, 16. Overenyie, 17. Impunge, 19. Asloun, 21. Cheer, 23. Pele.

42

ACROSS: 1. Salisbury Crags, 9. Mened, 10. Dirt-fleer, 11. Duns Scotus. 12. Chic, 14. New Elgin, 16. Starav, 18. Cotter, 19. Glen Neil, 21. Aros, 22. Tynecastle, 25. Epistle to, 26. Iorsa, 27. Inverleith Park.

DOWN: 1. St. Medan's Chapel, 2. Lunan, 3. Side-siller, 4. Undoomis, 5. Yarnut, 6. Reft, 7. Gi'en horse, 8. Brockville Park, 13. Stand Atish, 15. Watsonian, 17. Alberoni, 20. Oykell, 23. Torsa, 24. Stue.

43

ACROSS: 1. Dumbarton Youth, 9. Castlemilk, 10. Shim, 12. Behad, 13. Vivual, 16. Cuit, 17. The Cooper o', 19. Risp Grains, 20. Texa, 22. Ninian, 23. Usury, 26. Caho, 27. Cheese-hake, 28. Newbigging Farm.

DOWN: 2. Unst, 3. Balbeg, 4. Ramsay Head, 5. Ools, 6. Unhousened, 7. Hamilton Accies, 8. Scotichronicon, 11. Simon, 14. Wilson Shaw, 15. Achnasheen, 18. Ogham, 21. Crieff, 24. Shug, 25. Marr.

44

ACROSS: 1. Whitefoord House, 9. Leswalt, 10. Supping, 11. Aron, 12. Shoot, 13. In wi', 16. Exhoust, 17. Draatch, 18. Ordhead, 21. Growsin, 23. Urie, 24. Gaels, 25. Aits, 28. Elswick, 29. Patullo, 30. The Three Estates.

DOWN: 1. Wallace Monument, 2. Inshoch, 3. Egal, 4. Outshot, 5. Respond, 6. Hope, 7. Union St. 8. English and Scots, 14. Humet, 15. Saxon, 19. Dairsie, 20. Draukie, 21. Golspie, 22. Skillet, 26. Nith, 27. Stot.

45

ACROSS: 1. Cahute, 4. Black Law, 10. Spittal, 11. Croupie, 12. Fael, 13. Birdoswald, 16. Ruh-hed, 17. Borough, 20. Burnton, 21. Estlar, 24. Glen Rinnes, 25. Isle, 27. The Fair, 29. Outside, 30. Nearness, 31. Criest.

DOWN: 1. Cessford, 2. Hailes House, 3. Tite, 5. Loch Doon, 6. Crosshouse, 7. Lep, 8. Wields, 9. Alwin, 14. Argyllshire, 15. Ben Narnain, 18. Corn-arks, 19. Greement, 22. Ogston, 23. Devon, 26. Stur, 28. Eva.

46

ACROSS: 1. Lord Reith, 6. Sappy, 9. Nicol, 10. Ledington, 11. Ream-pig, 12. Ireland, 14. Sutherland, 15. Asti, 18. Iona, 19. Allan Wells, 23. Evanton, 25. Wall-tea, 26. Rathillet, 27. Ishes, 28. Ernit, 29. Para Handy.

DOWN: 1. Lanarkshire, 2. Riccarton, 3. Relapser, 4. Illegal, 5. Hadrian, 6. Singer, 7. Patna, 8. Yon, 13. Deil's Causey, 16. Splatchen, 17. Swillish, 20. Lang-lip, 21. Ae Water, 22. Strict, 24. Ayton, 26. Rae.

47

ACROSS: 3. Calton Hill, 8. Strath, 9. Alec, 10. Stevenston, 11. Hen, 13. Shol, 14. Gullane, 15. Sorn, 17. Smith, 20. Wierd, 22. Dips, 24. Trondra, 25. Foor, 27. Rae, 28. King Duncan, 29. Vane, 30. Abrede, 31. Norman's Law.

DOWN: 1. Stitchum, 2. Darvel, 3. Chandos, 4. Leith, 5. Oban, 6. Inchcape, 7. Loanhead, 12. Blaw, 14. Gnap, 16. Osda, 17. St. Ternan, 18. Iron-ever, 19. Hide, 21. Reodaide, 23. Skiddaw, 25. Fintry, 26. Snell, 28. Kean.

48

ACROSS: 1. West-bow, 5. Head Cut, 9. Skien, 10. Cardoness, 11. Strick, 12. Borderer, 14. Upgae, 15. Towiemore, 18. Dunallant, 20. Essie, 22. Bowdings, 24. Swykes, 26. Studderts, 27. Tylie, 28. Tennant, 29. Norland.

DOWN: 1. West Sound, 2. Slitrig, 3. Ben Screel, 4. Wick, 5. Heriot-Watt, 6. Amond, 7. Cheerio, 8. Tiser. 13. St. Margaret, 16. Ewes Water, 17. Edenshead, 19. Newburn, 21. St. Kilda, 22. Beset, 23. India, 25. Usan.

49

ACROSS: 1. Monimail, 5. Aboyne, 9. Dryburgh, 10. Ding up, 12. Alastrean, 14. Nimmo, 15. Sim, 16. Bought, 19. Eance, 22. Abash, 23. Strake, 25. Ilk, 28. Leill, 29. Inchkeith, 32. Tottie, 33. Maryhill, 34. Renown, 35. Sleenger.

DOWN: 1. Madras, 2. Naysay, 3. Mount, 4. Ingle, 6. Brian Meek, 7. Yagiment, 8. Explorer, 11. Anster, 13. Rhu, 17. Ochilview, 18. Gaskin, 20. Ballater, 21. Hamilton, 24. Ash, 26. Fiking, 27. Choler, 30. Crail, 31. Keyse.

50

ACROSS: 1. Paddy Meehan, 9. Mary, 10. Cockenheugh, 11. Ugie, 14. Chasers, 17. Udall, 18. Tatch, 19. Elder, 20. Neese, 21. Over a', 22. Sithe, 23. Insch, 24. Siler, 25. Strathy, 29. Lare, 32. Rowardennan, 33. Naip, 34. Green Tables.

DOWN: 2. Avon, 3. Dyke, 4. Minch, 5. Evens, 6. Aiger, 7. Margot Wells, 8. Byre Theatre, 12. Burntisland, 13. Ravenscraig, 14. Cleeshs, 15. Eadie, 16. Strousy, 19. Etter, 26. Thoor,27. Alane, 28. Had at, 30. Snab, 31. Hale.

51

ACROSS: 1. Drumclog, 5. Acharn, 9. Neidpath, 10. Cowdaw, 11. Eyemouth, 12. Ower wi', 14. An Teallach, 18. Druim Dearg, 22. Liddle, 23. Essonyie, 24. Enacts, 25. Apotheck, 26. Soking, 27. Glen Isla.

DOWN: 1 & 2. Dundee United, 3. Capoot, 4. Outstander, 6. Cromwell, 7. Alderman, 8. New Light, 13. Ben Resipol, 15. Udallers, 16. Bund-sack, 17. Embleton, 19. Morton, 20. Lyness, 21. Benk wa'.

52

ACROSS: 7. Paisley Pirates, 9. Snacky, 10. Eskadale, 11. Sika deer, 13. Ormond, 14. Eger, 15. Broom, 16. Mool, 17. Tarbat, 19. Harp Rock, 21. Aggreges, 23. Priest, 24. Repenting Stool.

DOWN: 1. Spinning Maggie, 2. Sinclair, 3. Cloyte, 4. Wyre, 5. Kirkcolm, 6. Dardrum, 8. Eglinton Castle, 12. Rioch, 15. Bathgate, 16. Morrison, 18. Barren, 20. Repose, 22. Syne.

53

ACROSS: 1. Starav, 5. Teviot, 8. Irony, 9. Rimmer, 10. Turner, 11. Grawl, 14. Goblin Ha', 16. Rogers, 18. Highland Society, 20. Set-aff, 22. Neilston, 25 & 27. Raith Rovers, 28. Ardeer, 29. Annan, 30. Ellary, 31. Temple.

DOWN: 1. Sproug, 2. Arms, 3. Virginia, 4. Royal and Ancient, 5. Tytler, 6. Iona, 7. Terris, 12. All-heal, 13. Against, 15. Opine, 17. Ratho, 19. Oliphant, 20. Sorrie, 21. Forsay, 23. Nairne, 24. Evil, 26. Kemp.

54

ACROSS: 1. Killiecrankie, 10. Ingangs, 11. Beer-can, 12. Haar, 13. Diary, 14. Syne, 17. Glencoe, 18. Onthank, 19. Falloch, 22. Ben Ledi, 24. Aird, 25. Lyall, 26. Fash, 29. Estover, 30. Rickman, 31. Holyroodhouse.

DOWN: 2. Ingrate, 3. Lang, 4. Erskine, 5. Roberto, 6. Neep, 7. Inchyra, 8. Sir Hugh Fraser, 9. Inverkeithing, 15. Scoot, 16. Stone, 20. Loretto. 21. Hay-broo, 22. Baldred, 23. Erasmus, 27. Ivry, 28. Echo.

55

ACROSS: 1. Drumnavick, 6. Isla, 9. Invergarry, 10. Bril, 12. Sheena Easton, 15. Fair Eliza, 17. Roche, 18. Endow, 19. Glentrool, 20. Sir R(obert) Clifford, 24. Aven, 25. St. Finichan, 26. Gask, 27. Inchbrakie.

DOWN: 1. Deil, 2. Ulva, 3. North Berwick, 4. Veage, 5. Carradale, 7. Strath Croe, 8. Allan Wells, 11. Cairn Terrier, 13. Afterstang, 14. Wilderness, 16. Ingliston, 21. Frith, 22. Chak, 23. Anne.

56

ACROSS: 1. Caledonian Canal, 6. Glas, 10. See 1 across, 11. West Haven, 12. Graymeal, 13. Nanna, 15. Hoddler, 17. Glen App, 19. Raeburn Place, 21. Uplands, 22. Beith, 24. Carntyne, 27. Ebionitic, 28. See 19 across, 29. Dale, 30. Restenneth.

DOWN: 1. Cock, 2. Longridge, 3. Dalry, 4. New Year, 5. Assilag, 7. Leven, 8. Sunday Post, 9. Shinwell, 14. Shortbread, 16. Laughing, 18. Annandale, 20. Nochtie, 21. Upricht, 23. Idill, 25. Typin', 26. Pech.

57

ACROSS: 1. Glasgow Rangers, 9. Rikki, 10. St. Malachi, 11. Old Meldrum, 12. Pauw, 14. St. Manire, 16. Lintel, 18. Relate, 19. Alliance, 21. Croy, 22. Scots Greys, 25. Almondale, 26. Tirl o', 27. William Tennant.

DOWN: 1. Gordon Strachan, 2. Asked, 3. Guinea-note, 4. Wash-dirt, 5. Armour, 6. Galt, 7. Riccarton, 8. Sir Walter Scott, 13. Livingston, 15. Malcolm II, 17. Plattest, 20. Achara, 23. Eorsa, 24. Anil.

58

ACROSS: 1. Kyle of Lochalsh, 9. Loch Ericht, 10. Snug, 12. Gight, 13. Barrel, 16. Wood, 17. Livingston, 19. Thriepland, 20. Aesc, 22. Rachan, 23. Small, 26. Orra, 27. Struie Hill, 28. Treshnish Isles.

DOWN: 2. Yack, 3. Eredin, 4. Faichfield, 5. Ocht, 6. Lintrathen, 7. Highland Cattle, 8. Blackwaterfoot, 11. Largs, 14. Corrachree, 15. Lion's Mouth, 18. Dewar, 21. Alness, 24. Etui, 25. Fife.

59

ACROSS: 1. Bunloit, 5. Affects, 9. Angus, 10. Ardersier, 11. Mull, 12. Stook, 13. And I, 16. Rubha, 18. Rusky Loch, 20. Speymouth, 23. Immer, 25. Unco, 26. Rammy, 27. Shee, 31. Heartland, 32. Minto, 33. Narside, 34. New Deer.

DOWN: 1. Braemar, 2 & 4. Nigel Tranter, 3. Ooss, 4. See 2 down, 5. Ardross, 6. Ford, 7. Cairngorm, 8. Skreigh, 14. Kaims, 15. Tyrie, 17. Breacharr, 19. Ult, 20. Sauchen, 21. Ugadale, 22. Hampden, 24. Raemoir, 28. Henge, 29. Etui, 30. Smow.

60

ACROSS: 1. Granite City, 9. Hugo, 10. Sauchiehall, 11. Sned, 14. Brooked, 17. Rooer, 18. Union, 19. See 14 down, 20. Sclat, 21. Silit, 22. Inver, 23. Rykes, 24. Agnew, 25. Hotchen, 29. Ushy, 32. Strathallan, 33. Gawk, 34. Skibo Castle.

DOWN: 1. Ryan, 2. Nick, 4. Trier, 5. Cahoo, 6. Tylie, 7. Burntisland, 8. Gordonstown, 12. Fraserburgh, 13. Pollok-shaws, 14. British linen, 15. Kaner, 16. Dunstan, 19. Lovat, 26. Ontak, 27. Clamb, 28. Ethic, 30 & 31. Glas Maol.